PRE - 1940
TRIUMPH
MOTOR CARS
from
FAMILY PHOTOGRAPH
ALBUMS

Volume 2

Written and
compiled by
Graham Shipman

Published by
Graham Shipman
Brick Kiln Farm
Shropham
Attleborough
Norfolk
NR17 1ED

Printed by
Postprint
Taverner House
Harling Road
East Harling
Norfolk
NR16 2QR

First published in May 2010

British Library Cataloguing-in-Publication Data:
A catalogue record for this book is available from the British Library.

ISBN 978-0-9550422-2-5

Mixed Sources
Product group from well-managed forests and other controlled sources
www.fsc.org Cert no. TT-COC-003067
© 1996 Forest Stewardship Council

FSC

The trademark of the Forest Stewardship Council (FSC) guarantees that the wood pulp used to make this paper comes from forests which are well managed according to strict environmental, social and economic standards.

This, my second book, on gathering together memories of life with these early Triumph cars, is dedicated to the memory of a dear friend, Morris Phelan.

We first met in the 1990s through being members of the Pre-1940 Triumph Owners Club and our friendship developed. As both Archivist and Registrar for the club I recognised that many amusing and interesting stories were to be told and Morris, with his printing and publishing business, happily volunteered his services and was instrumental in guiding me through all the processes necessary to bring my first volume to fruition. Without him the path would have been much more difficult.

Morris was a busy, enthusiastic man, fiercely keen on his Triumph hobby whose generosity spread to the publication of our club's magazine. He freely gave his expertise and the services of his company to enable members to enjoy a bi-monthly magazine which would be the envy of most clubs. What we learnt from him is continued to this day.

Lasting memories for many club members are of Morris and his wife Carol arriving at rallies and events in their small and much loved Super Seven. Their arrival was always accompanied by lots of arm waving and broad smiles and they both played a great part in the social side of our gatherings. Morris is pictured above (on the right) standing next to his beloved car and talking to Alan Davis (ex-Chairman and now Honorary Member of the club – *see page 105 for Alan's first Dolomite*).

It was the greatest of shocks when the sad news came that Morris had died whilst on holiday in Spain with Carol. His funeral at Derby Cathedral will always be remembered as a fitting tribute to a man that so many loved and now miss.

It was a pleasure and a privilege to have known him.

Acknowledgements

This style of book would be impossible to publish without the generous help from all its contributors. Therefore I wish to initially thank everyone who took the time to write down their Triumph memories and trust me with their irreplaceable photographs. Often these photographs were not readily to hand and typically required some searching through boxes in the attic or asking other family members if they had any photographs tucked away.

Being able to contact so many people with a Triumph history was in no doubt helped by my role as Archivist and Registrar for the Pre-1940 Triumph Owners Club. I am sure that it also helped with publishing my appeals for memories and photographs in newspapers and motoring journals. I thank the club for their full support during the five years it has taken to gather together enough stories to publish this book.

I also wish to thank fellow club members Bernhard Ruest (Switzerland), Andrew Scott (Scotland), John Shepherd (Australia), David Thomas (Portugal), Dale Will (USA) and the many club members in England for finding past Triumph owners which have helped make this book truly 'global'.

A special thanks goes to my aunt Iris (my father's sister) with her interest in genealogy. This resulted in her tracking down Hazel Jenkins in Northumberland. Hazel is the granddaughter of John (known as Jack to his family and friends) Shipman, my great uncle, who owned a Gloria from the 1930s to the 1950s. It is partially due to hearing family stories of great-uncle Jack and his Gloria that got me interested in Triumph motor cars. Our two sides of the family lost touch over 30 years ago and all I had as a reminder of his Gloria was a brief snippet of movie film of it travelling up my grandparents' drive. Therefore, I think you can imagine how surprised and pleased I was when, via Iris, I received photographs (on my birthday of all days!) of him, his wife Liley, and daughter Joan with the Gloria! So good was one of the photographs that it immediately became my obvious choice for this book's front cover (*you can read Hazel's memories on page 26*). One of the many coincidences that occurred while writing this book was when I entered his Gloria in the club's register. To my surprise it had already been entered in the early 1960s when owned by Mr Instone from Slough, who was probably the person that great-uncle Jack had sold it to!

Thanks go to my friends and fellow Triumph enthusiasts Edna and Roger Barnes for proof reading the many drafts. It is with their considerable enthusiastic help and encouragement that this book has been as enjoyable to publish as the first volume.

Finally, I wish to acknowledge the help I received with the book's production from Jeremy Warren and Robbie Rees at Postprint.

Some of the happiest and most rewarding years of my working life were those I spent as the founder editor of *Triumph World* magazine from 1995 to 2007. Launching a new motoring magazine is always a very speculative venture, and producing one about a marque which had disappeared over a decade earlier was quite a risk, but the enthusiastic reception that the first issue received made all the hard work worthwhile. The continued success of the publication was also most gratifying.

I am particularly proud of the fact that, during my tenure as editor, the magazine was able to substantially increase awareness of early Triumph cars and the history associated with them, and participating in a number of Pre-1940 Triumph Owners Club rallies, where I could examine these marvellous cars close-up and get to know the owners, were personal highlights. I believe it was at one such event that I first met Graham Shipman.

One of an editor's perks is receiving advance copies of newly published books to review. Now motoring titles tend to fall into one of several categories – make or model history, restoration guide, workshop manual, modification or tuning data, etc – but when Graham's first volume of family photographs arrived on my desk it was immediately obvious that he had created a very special book indeed.

Five years later he has put together a second volume of equally outstanding quality. Once again using old photos that would normally be hidden away in albums or boxes and combining them with personal stories and brief historical details, he has produced another fascinating book that provides a unique look at pre-war Triumph cars and the social context of the periods they existed in.

As I wrote in my 2005 review: "I can think of no higher praise than to say that I wish it was my name on the front cover rather than his!" That sentiment also applies to the book you now hold in your hands and while my name may not be on the cover, thanks to Graham's generosity I can at least claim to have contributed a small part of the contents.

A Brief History of Triumph

Triumph was established in Coventry during 1887 by Siegfried Bettmann, a German immigrant. Initially producing bicycles and then motorcycles, Triumph gained a reputation for high quality well engineered products during the First World War. Triumph entered the field of motor car manufacture in 1923, following the purchase of the Dawson Car Company in Clay Lane, Coventry.

Triumph's first three motor car models were of high quality and often more expensive than their rivals but offered that little bit extra. The 13/35 model was the first British car to have hydraulic brakes. It wasn't until the introduction of the Super Seven that Triumph produced cars in higher numbers, approximately 15,000. These Super Sevens were of conventional design offering the motoring public an upmarket alternative to the popular Austin Sevens. The Super Sevens were produced between 1927 and 1932, a large number of these being exported to Australia in rolling chassis form.

In 1933 Bettmann retired at the age of 70 and Lt. Col. Claude Holbrook was appointed to take over the reins. It was at this time Triumph decided to move up from the small to the medium sporting car market. This put them in direct competition with the likes of Riley and SS (later to be renamed Jaguar). Frank Warner, their in-house designer, came up with the Gloria, a handsome rakish car in either saloon or open form, mounted on an underslung chassis. Also at this time to gain an even more sporting pedigree Triumph offered Donald Healey, well known for his successes in rallying motor cars including Super Sevens, the position of Experimental Manager. Healey's appointment was made just prior to the Glorias' launch and within a year he had been promoted to Technical Director.

Glorias soon gained a good reputation and by 1935 Triumph offered over 25 different models. They sold well but were very expensive to produce and this took its toll on finances, culminating in the sale of the profitable motorcycle business to Mr Sangster (of Ariel Motorcycles) in 1936. With this cash injection from the motorcycle business it gave Triumph the finance to develop their new Dolomite and Vitesse models, styled by Walter Belgrove.

By 1939 Triumph's finances were again in a very poor state, resulting in the business being sold by the receivers (Gibson & Ashford) to Thomas Ward Ltd., who oversaw the production of the last few Dolomites and Triumph's final model the Twelve Saloon. Car production ceased in 1940. The final 'nail in the coffin' took place in November 1940 when the Triumph works were destroyed, along with all the records, during a German air raid on Coventry.

Between 1923 and 1940 Triumph's total production is estimated at 35,000 cars of all models, which is less than a large motor car manufacturer, such as Morris, would produce in one year.

After the war the Standard Motor Company bought the Triumph name. Standard's policy was then to badge their upmarket and sports models as Triumphs. Walter Belgrove (now having joined Standard's team of stylists) was to be the only tangible connection with the old Triumph company.

This book's background

Following the success of my first book, with its emphasis on life with a Triumph motor car rather than their technical aspects, I was encouraged to embark on this matching second volume. Not surprisingly this book has taken over twice as long to complete compared with the first. I have found it a greater challenge, as the years roll on, to find people who can remember travelling in these pre-war Triumphs. It is now 70 years since the last car left the original Triumph company factory.

It has been tremendously rewarding contacting and corresponding with the contributors, during which several coincidences occurred. On two occasions the same car is featured during different periods of ownership (*see pages 51, 52 and 81, 82*) without the knowledge of the other past owners!

Another coincidence occurred just after I had returned home after recording 'Coventry registered' Triumphs from Coventry's archives, held in the Herbert Gallery. I received an email from Barry Vaudin (*see page 56*) mentioning that his father owned a very rare Triumph and did the club know anything about it. Well, its registration was one of those I had recorded that day, so I could happily tell him all about this car including the last owner's name, which was his father's! I was also able to inform Barry that his father's car was originally owned by Triumph and featured in advertisements published in *The Autocar* magazine.

The final coincidence was very similar to that of Barry's but this time it involved Eric Whitehouse and his Dolomite (*see page 110*). I had already received Eric's contribution when fellow club member Steve Jacobs completed his search through Doncaster's archives for Triumphs registered in that area. Amongst them was Eric's Dolomite and from its newly received details I learnt that it was a very rare variant and also what became of this car after Eric's ownership. Its fate was of particular interest to my father Jack and his brother Doug, (both 'old car' enthusiasts) as it had been broken up in a scrapyard situated along the same road as their family's metal finishing business!

Introduction

In the first book, published in June 2005, I mentioned that the club had recorded 1,500 Triumph vehicles in their Register. Since then the number has more than doubled to over 3,400. This is largely due to club members, including myself, recently gaining access to county registration records for the years between 1923 and 1940. Therefore it is worth noting that the recorded numbers stated for individual models has significantly increased in this second volume.

I am pleased with the spread of models featured in this book. It represents a good and varied selection of Triumph's popular models, plus some rare variants too. I hope that when reading these personal accounts of life with these Triumphs, during the period when they were 'everyday cars', you find it entertaining, interesting and nostalgic.

———

Graham Shipman
Norfolk
May 2010

PRE - 1940
TRIUMPH
MOTOR CARS
from
FAMILY PHOTOGRAPH
ALBUMS

Volume 2

Specification

Engine: 10.20 hp;
4 cylinders; 63.5 mm bore
by 110 mm stroke: capacity
1,393 cc; side valves; single
Zenith carburettor.
Gearbox: 4 forward speeds
and reverse.
Brakes: Drum brakes; rod
operated on rear wheels
only.
Track: 3 ft. 10 in.
Wheelbase: 8 ft. 6 in.
Production: April 1923 to
January 1926
Price New: £420

Featured Car

Registration Number:
JS ????
Licensing Authority:
Ross-shire
Registration Date:
1926
Notes: This, one of two
recorded, is the only
photographic proof the club
has received that Triumph
actually made this tourer
model. There are two
10/20s surviving, one 2/3-
Seater All-Weather model
in excellent original un-
restored condition and one
restored Sports model.
This featured car no longer
exists.

10/20 4-SEATER TOURER

My life long interest in cars started in 1926 when I was eight years old. It was then that my father bought this Triumph new from Mackay's Garage, Dingwall. The photograph was taken in April or May 1926 and features (from left to right) my cousin, sisters, father, brother and myself with the car parked outside my cousin's house at Big Sand, Gairloch. The house is now owned by my son.

Undoubtedly father's choice of car stemmed from his earlier association with Triumph motorcycles which he found to be excellent trouble free machines. Happily the car proved to be no exception apart from being prone to rear spring breakage. Father always carried a block of wood as a 'get you home' measure. A crucial part of the car on hilly West Highland gravel roads (no tarmac then) was the two wheel braking system, which though effective, had to be frequently adjusted.

Common to cars from that era the engine was decarbonized and valves re-ground every 10,000 miles or so. I well remember my astonishment on seeing the engine in bits and asking father (a born mechanic and just as well since we lived 70 miles from the nearest garage) if he could put it back together again!

The gear change (four speed and reverse) and handbrake were on the right, a fairly standard layout then and an arrangement which gave an uncluttered central passage.

At a very early age my greatest joy was to start the Triumph in the morning and drive it out of the garage ready for father to proceed on his journey. Soon I was driving on the largely deserted roads, apart from sheep, having learned to control my excitement and the fierce clutch!

Father kept the Triumph for four years before selling it to a nephew for £50 who subsequently passed it on to a cousin. He had the misfortune to break down between Ullapool and Garve. Returning the next day he discovered to his dismay that deer had descended overnight and eaten the car's hood! Sadly it was scrapped shortly thereafter.

Duncan Mackenzie, Ross-shire

FIFTEEN COACHBUILT SALOON

Specification

Engine: 15 hp; 4 cylinders; 77.5 mm bore by 115 mm stroke: capacity 2,169 cc; side valves; single Zenith carburettor.
Gearbox: 3 forward speeds and reverse.
Brakes: Lockheed hydraulically operated on all four wheels: transmission handbrake.
Track: 4 ft. 8¾ in.
Wheelbase: 9 ft. 4 in.
Production: February 1926 to 1929
Price New: £495

Featured Car

Registration Number: ER 8818
Licensing Authority: Cambridgeshire
Registration Date: 1928
Notes: 33 Fifteen saloons of various styles have been recorded. This car still survives in fine condition and is the only four-door saloon known to exist. Its coachwork was built by Hancock & Warman Ltd., in Coventry. A similar Fifteen saloon survives but is a two-door fabric bodied model.

On my way home one weekend in 1959 I saw this car at a garage near Cambridge and being interested I stopped to look at it. It was painted battleship grey with a black radiator shell. The garage proprietor told me that the owner had recently died and it was for sale at £50. It still had a 1935 licence disc affixed to the windscreen. All he would tell me about the deceased owner was that he spent a lot of time abroad in the car's early years and had put the car up on blocks in December 1935 which explained why it had only covered 4,290 miles. The car had then been left to his chauffeur.

I was interested in buying the car so after a cursory pre-sale inspection, including filling the radiator with water which immediately reappeared under the car, I managed to negotiate the price down to £45. I returned to collect the car with my brother and a Land-Rover to tow the car home. The brakes did not work because the fluid had solidified so we had to rely on the feeble transmission brake. After being towed a few miles we were forced to stop because one of the tyres was smoking! It had started to melt so we swapped it for the spare. By the time we had got home another two had gone the same way despite keeping our speed down to 20 mph.

Re-commissioning the car back on the road was reasonably straightforward and I used it as my everyday transport right up to 1972. The black radiator surround proved to be dirt and with a lot of cleaning and polishing it came up like new and in 1963 I repainted the body blue and black.

When I bought the car I was a land agent dealing with agricultural estates in Market Harborough and St Albans. I would drive the car to work at the start of the week, travel around the estates I was looking after, then drive it back to my home in Essex for the weekend. During these thirteen years and 20,000 miles it only had to be towed home once when the magneto failed.

Since 1972 the car has led a gentler life and is now only driven to shows and rallies. This photograph was taken at Silverstone on 14th April 1962.

Michael Cooke, Essex

Specification

Engine: 7.9 hp; 4 cylinders; 56.5 mm bore by 83 mm stroke: capacity 832.24 cc; side valves; single Solex carburettor.

Gearbox: 3 forward speeds and reverse.

Brakes: Lockheed hydraulically operated on all four wheels; transmission handbrake.

Track: 3 ft. 6 in.

Wheelbase: 6 ft. 9 in.

Production: February to December 1928

Price New: £182.10s

Featured Car

Registration Number: RF 4749

Licensing Authority: Staffordshire

Registration Date: 1928

Notes: 24 have been recorded and none survive. Donald Healey (who later worked for Triumph) completed the 1929 Monte Carlo Rally in a car of the same type.

SUPER SEVEN COACHBUILT SALOON

It must have been in the mid 1960s that I noticed this Triumph parked in front of a house in Nuneaton, as illustrated in this photograph. Incidentally, two doors away was parked an AJS Two Seater Tourer; I wonder how many of those have survived?

Through a mutual friend I learnt that this Triumph was for sale. The owner, who worked at the Motor Industries Research Association (MIRA), invited me with two friends of his to go for a spin in her, during the course of which I found myself travelling up the A5 at a terrifying speed of 55 mph! The owner and I agreed on the princely sum of £50 and she was mine. I intended her as a second car, since I had to travel 20 miles to work in those days, with no alternative mode of transport available.

The only major repair I carried out on her was the overhaul of the clutch and flywheel. The starter motor had worn away the teeth on the flywheel so I had these welded up and re-profiled. For some reason I continued to prefer cranking the engine by hand. Driving the Triumph was always great fun, but she needed to be handled with respect. One didn't take liberties with the steering, suspension etc. and if you hadn't mastered the art of the crash gearbox you were soon the subject of unwanted attention!

She was a reliable little car and must have been desirable in her pre-war days. There was no water pump or fuel pump, the tank being mounted behind the bulkhead feeding the carburettor by gravity. Her one advanced feature was four wheel hydraulic brakes and very efficient they were too. The track rod ends were spring loaded which was a feature my local MoT operative simply couldn't understand. Inside, the seats and trim, including the dashboard, were covered in a pale green plush material. There were no locks fitted!

After about four years use I intended to restore her, but I soon came to realise that this would be impossible unless I could keep her under cover. So rather than letting her end up like my 1932 Lanchester 18 hp I reluctantly decided to sell her. Eventually I sold her for £55 to Robin Griffin of Blackfordby, Leicestershire, who also happened to work at MIRA. He wished to restore her, but I never heard any more from him. It is sad to think that she may no longer exist.

Roger Fifield, Warwickshire

SUPER SEVEN FABRIC SALOON

This photograph was taken during the mid-1930s outside the house of my grandparents, which they had built in 1934 in The Close, Saltwood, Kent (the house to their left was still being built). It pictures John Glendinning beside his Triumph, who was the brother of an aunt by marriage. John is dressed in his Royal Navy uniform when he was a petty officer.

There is not much more that I can say about this photograph apart from that it was taken on a Kodak 'Box Brownie' Model C camera made in Canada between 1924 and 1935; this may interest the photographers amongst you.

It is a pity that this is the only photograph I have of John's Triumph as the number plate cannot be seen from the angle it has been taken. It is also not helped by the fact that the front number plate is mounted deep between the springs and chassis. It would have been interesting to know the car's registration number.

Paul Day, Hertfordshire

Specification

Engine: 7.9 hp; 4 cylinders; 56.5 mm bore by 83 mm stroke: capacity 832.24 cc; side valves; single Solex carburettor.
Gearbox: 3 forward speeds and reverse.
Brakes: Lockheed hydraulically operated on all four wheels; transmission handbrake.
Track: 3 ft. 6 in.
Wheelbase: 6 ft. 9 in.
Production: September 1929 to August 1930
Price New: £182.10s

Featured Car

Registration Number: Unknown
Licensing Authority: Unknown
Registration Date: Unknown
Notes: 24 have been recorded and one survives in fine restored condition. This car no longer exists.

Specification

Engine: 7.9 hp; 4 cylinders; 56.5 mm bore by 83 mm stroke: capacity 832.24 cc; side valves; single Solex carburettor (now fitted with an updraft Zenith).

Gearbox: 3 forward speeds and reverse.

Brakes: Lockheed hydraulically operated on all four wheels; transmission handbrake.

Track: 3 ft. 6 in.

Wheelbase: 6 ft. 9 in. (extended to 7 ft. 9 in. to allow for the fitting of the Alvis body).

Production: September 1929 to August 1930

Price New: £182.10s

Featured Car

Registration Number: VU 1526

Licensing Authority: Manchester

Registration Date: November 1930

Notes: This Super Seven, which was originally a Fabric Saloon the same as featured on page 4, was bought new from David Rosenfield Ltd., Victoria Street, Manchester.

SUPER SEVEN FABRIC SALOON (converted to a Tourer)

I bought this, my first car, when I was sixteen in 1962, from a Mr Gittins of West Kirby, Wirral, who kept it untaxed under a canvas sheet in West Kirby railway yard. At that time I contacted a Mr Ryder its first post-war owner who told me some of its history. The car was laid-up in Birkenhead during the war and was badly burned when its garage was set alight during an incendiary raid on Liverpool. Mr Ryder bought the car in 1948, discarded the fire damaged Triumph body and replaced it with one from a scrapped Alvis Silver Eagle. After some modifications the body fitted well and he just managed to finish rebuilding it the day before his wedding. Unfortunately the body was now a couple of inches wider, so he had to knock down the dividing wall between his driveway and the neighbours to get the car out of the garage and onto the road! Thankfully his untested car gave no trouble on honeymoon and he sold it eight years later in 1957.

A school friend told me that this old car could be bought cheaply and thought it would be ideal to learn to drive around our field, so I parted with £5 and it was towed home in the rain by my very patient parents, with no hood or wipers and the handbrake being the only means of stopping! I spent the next two years tinkering with it and eventually rebuilt it for when I passed my driving test.

I used the car to go to work and for local trips all summer without any weather equipment until my father rather strangely asked if he could borrow it to go to his work in Liverpool. He returned that night with a brand new hood and side screens. I was of course over the moon and mightily impressed that he had driven my very ancient little car through the Mersey Tunnel in the rush hour, twice!

I used the car for two years and the only time it let me down was on the way to Llangollen when the magneto gave up and my long suffering father towed me some 30 miles home. I eventually sold it to an acquaintance when I went to agricultural college and bought a Dellow. He had aspirations beyond the car's capabilities, so I bought it back a year later and stored it in my parents' garage while away at university in North Wales.

I married Jane in 1972 and considered selling it again, but she thought I would regret the decision and insisted I keep it. When we moved to Stratford in 1979 it was trailered down from Cheshire and has remained in a barn since.

I have now been spurred on to restore this much neglected but still basically sound car to a roadworthy condition. One day Jane may actually experience 'Super Seven motoring' – it is the very least she deserves!

Peter Beeley, Warwickshire

SUPER SEVEN SPORTS

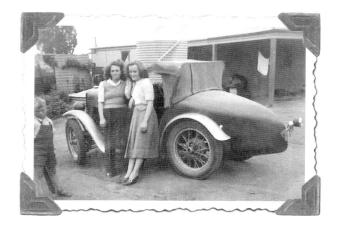

Specification

Engine: 7.9 hp; 4 cylinders; 56.5 mm bore by 83 mm stroke: capacity 832.24 cc; side valves; single Solex carburettor.
Gearbox: 3 forward speeds and reverse.
Brakes: Lockheed hydraulically operated on all four wheels; transmission handbrake.
Track: 3 ft. 6 in.
Wheelbase: 6 ft. 9 in.
Production: September 1929 to August 1931
Price New: £265 Australian

Featured Car

Registration Number: Unknown
Licensing Authority: Unknown
Registration Date: 1930
Notes: Triumph exported Super Sevens to Australia as 'rolling chassis' which were then bodied by Australian coachbuilders. The body on this car may have been made by either Properts or Greens, who were located in Sydney. It cost £40 more than the the 'base' Two-Door Roadster model. (Australian Pounds were valued the same as British.) This car no longer exists.

In 1943, aged 20, I first saw and took a liking to this Super Seven. I remember it parked in a street looking quite dirty and dilapidated. I was stationed at an army camp in Cowra, west of Sydney. I had little money and my army pay was 6/6d per day but I plucked up courage to approach the owner, who wanted £40 for it, even though the engine was worn out. Still keen, I sold my 1929 500cc Matchless motorcycle for £35 and a deal was struck for the car.

I put it into a local garage and there it sat until the war finished. When I received my deferred pay the motor was rebuilt by them at a cost of £38. By now I had got married to a girl from a nearby town; the girl in the photo with the slacks standing with her sister and brother. The photo was taken in the back yard of her parents' home. At that time we had a 2½ year-old daughter and a new baby boy.

After the war I went back to my old job at Strathfield Body Works in Sydney. During these early post-war years it was difficult, if not impossible, to buy anything related to the car, but I still decided to renovate 'Trumpy'. The tyres were replaced with motorcycle tyres and I stripped the body back to its metal. This was in a terrible mess as the 'beetle back' was hand beaten and rough, so I spent a couple of weeks getting it smooth. I bought some beautiful blue leather to re-trim the interior and fitted a 1934 Dodge dashboard and instruments.

In 1947 we moved back to my home town of Goulburn. The only job I could find was digging a waterline trench with a pick and shovel, but I was soon promoted to chainman. While at work a cement truck reversed into Trumpy, which put it off the road for months while I repaired it.

When our third baby came along in 1953, I reluctantly had to sell Trumpy to buy a larger car, a 1932 Citroën. It had served us well and I later heard that the young fellow who bought Trumpy drove it 4,000 miles to Western Australia and then back to South Australia with no trouble.

Ossie Walsh, Queensland, Australia

Specification

Engine: 7.9 hp; 4 cylinders; 56.5 mm bore by 83 mm stroke: capacity 832.24 cc; side valves; single Solex carburettor.

Gearbox: 3 forward speeds and reverse.

Brakes: Lockheed hydraulically operated on all four wheels; transmission handbrake.

Track: 3 ft. 6 in.

Wheelbase: 6 ft. 9 in.

Production: September 1929 to August 1930

Price New: £167.10s

Featured Car

Registration Number: UW 3199

Licensing Authority: London

Registration Date: October or November 1929

Notes: 25 have been recorded and four still survive with their original style bodywork. This body style continued unchanged to July 1932. This is the first version, identified by the headlamps fitted low between the front wings. This car no longer exists.

My first car was this Super Seven. I bought it for £40 in 1952 as a non-runner and assisted by a friend we pushed it three quarters of a mile to a garage I had rented. I could not keep it at home as my father's Hillman Ten (pictured above with my Triumph) occupied the family garage which was sited at the end of a shared drive and in those days it was not practical to keep a car on the road as side-lights had to be left on at night.

The reason that the car was a non-runner was due to a broken magneto. I soon remedied this problem by converting it to coil ignition. I made many other body, mechanical and electrical improvements including changing the wings, fitting larger headlamps, adjusting the steering box and fitting a home-made heater.

I went on holiday to Combe Martin in Devon with a friend and en route we were faced with climbing Porlock Hill in the little car. We had started our journey very early in the morning dressed in overcoats, hats, scarves and gloves to fight against the cold of open air motoring but by the time we got to Porlock it was a warm summer's day and we had removed our warm clothing which laid between us on the seat. On approaching the hill I asked my friend to jump out when the speed dropped too low. As he jumped out he also pulled out our discarded clothing. By the time he had gathered them up I was well up the hill and did not dare to stop for another half mile. After a long wait he eventually appeared with an armful of clothes and puffing and blowing from his climb! When he had regained his breath I had the cheek to ask him to take the photograph shown on the right.

I mainly used the Triumph to attend motor race meetings as either a spectator or marshal for the 500 Motor Club and can remember travelling to Boreham, Brighton, Castle Combe, Crystal Palace, Goodwood and Silverstone.

I eventually sold the Triumph, again for £40, in 1954 or 1955. Sometime later it was bought by a work colleague to learn to drive in and on at least one occasion I remember taking him out in it.

Lionel Reeves, Hertfordshire

SUPER SEVEN 2/4-SEATER TOURER

Specification

Engine: 7.9 hp; 4 cylinders; 56.5 mm bore by 83 mm stroke: capacity 832.24 cc; side valves; single Solex carburettor.
Gearbox: 3 forward speeds and reverse.
Brakes: Lockheed hydraulically operated on all four wheels; transmission handbrake.
Track: 3 ft. 6 in.
Wheelbase: 6 ft. 9 in.
Production: September 1930 to August 1931
Price New: £ 167.10s

Featured Car

Registration Number: GH 3949
Licensing Authority: London
Registration Date: 1930
Notes: 15 have been recorded and four still survive with their original style bodywork. This body style continued unchanged to July 1932. This is the second version, identified by the higher fitment of the headlamps. This car no longer exists.

While still a student I bought this secondhand Super Seven for £35 in 1934. Unusually it had both coil and magneto ignition, so it could be started (by handle) irrespective of the battery condition. To improve the lighting I fitted the larger plated headlamps.

The following year a fellow student and I optimistically decided on a European tour to include the Alps. With the invaluable 'Europa Touring' atlas and a sheaf of 'Carnets de passage en douane' we set off for Dover, where the little car was craned onto a ship for Ostend.

The new concrete dual carriageway from Ostend to Brussels did not prepare us for the dreadful bone-shaking cobbled roads to follow (pictured in the first photograph) but we managed to reach Bonn on the Rhine without incident. Here we made a diversion to the Nurburgring to see a bit of the German Grand Prix and to marvel at the skill and daring of such legendary drivers as Caracciola (Mercedes), Von Stuck (Auto Union) and Nuvolari (Alfa Romeo) controlling the raw power of their cars as they raced over the rally-like country roads of the 17 mile course.

From Bonn we roughly followed the Rhine until we left it to take in Heidelberg on our way to the Black Forest, whose peaceful beauty (second photograph) was in sharp contrast to the strident array of swastika flags and banners that smothered its streets. When we reached the western tip of Austria on Lake Constance we were once again keeping left, having switched road sides at the frontier.

On the way to Innsbruck we climbed our first alpine pass, the Arlberg, which immediately exposed a shortcoming of the radiator and fan cooling system that was to dog us all through the Alps. Lacking a pump, it could not cope with prolonged slow progress in low gear and we were constantly on the boil. Frequent stops were needed to cool off and replenish with water or melted snow.

Austria's newly opened magnificent Grossglockner pass lay between us and the Italian Dolomites and on completion of this we were given a large windscreen sticker. In Italy, again on the right, we climbed the passes of Pordoi, Falzarego and Stelvio (approximately 9,000 feet) with no more trouble than the ever present overheating. Dropping into Switzerland by way of the Umbrail and Ofen passes, we headed for Berne, completing our 'kill' of nine passes with the Fluela and Furka. Rough roads, steep hairpins and stiff gradients had not given the little car any problem; if only the cooling system had been as good!

After seeing the Swiss Grand Prix, it was time to head for home through eastern France as our finances were getting low. All went well until we ran a big end near Luxembourg and, unable to afford repairs, had to coax the car gently, freewheeling as much as possible, over the last 300 miles until we finally rattled into London with all four big ends gone!

This car served me well for 10,000 miles. I sold it for £25 in exchange for a 1932 Southern Cross Tourer.

Laurence Hole, Hertfordshire

Engine: 7.9 hp; 4 cylinders; 56.5 mm bore by 83 mm stroke: capacity 832.24 cc; side valves; single Solex carburettor.

Gearbox: 3 forward speeds and reverse.

Brakes: Lockheed hydraulically operated on all four wheels; transmission handbrake.

Track: 3 ft. 6 in.

Wheelbase: 6 ft. 9 in.

Production: September 1930 to August 1931

Price New: £167.10s

Featured Car

Registration Number: EP 4824

Licensing Authority: Montgomeryshire

Registration Date: October 1930

Notes: This body style was available from September 1929 to July 1932. This is the second version. The final version was fitted with a Scorpion style radiator surround, as can be seen on page 11 and could be ordered with a four forward speed gearbox.

This car still exists, but its condition is unknown.

SUPER SEVEN 2/4-SEATER TOURER

These photographs of my Super Seven with Pauline, my wife, pretending to drive and myself pretending to be a very nervous passenger were taken in 1960. We met because of the car when my friend, Mike Davies, and I were on holiday in Bournemouth in 1959. A certain young lady told us that our radiator was leaking and now here we are 47 years on with four children and seven lovely grandchildren! My word, how time passes.

The Super Seven was purchased from a man who lived in the village of Prees near Whitchurch, Salop. Mike and I bought it for £35, which was the going rate in those days for an 'old banger'. It was for sale because he was in need of a larger car for his growing family. We paid our £35 and drove it home. Later Mike, aged 21 years, had to go away to do his national service. He had what they called a Deferment, which meant he had to do three years instead of the usual time of two years if you commenced at 18 years of age. It was at this time that I suggested to him that I bought his share in the car, to which he agreed. He later went on to buy a more modern Ford Eight Popular which he thought would be more reliable for his trips home from the airbase.

Now that the car was wholly mine, Pauline and I went on holiday to Southsea and on our return journey had the rear differential pack up. I am afraid that for us this proved to be the demise of the car as spares were unheard of at that time, so it ended up in a scrapyard. I did hear that a student rescued it and it was later sold to a Mr Kane in Staffordshire. I believe his wife still has the car and that she was a member of the Pre-1940 Triumph Owners Club.

In 1978 I bought another Super Seven and have been busy restoring it back to its former glory with help from Dave Bucknall who is also a keen classic car enthusiast. Hopefully it should soon be finished and Pauline and I can relive our early motoring, but sadly this time without Mike as he passed away in January 2006. He was a true friend and was very supportive of my present Super Seven's restoration. I will miss him.

Horace Gibbs, Staffordshire

SCORPION SPORTS 2-SEATER DE LUXE

Specification

Engine: 11.85 hp;
6 cylinders; 56.5 mm bore
by 80 mm stroke; capacity
1,203 cc; side valves; single
carburettor.
Gearbox: 3 forward speeds
and reverse.
Brakes: Lockheed
hydraulically operated on all
four wheels; transmission
handbrake.
Track: 3 ft. 7½ in.
Wheelbase: 7 ft. 8¼ in.
Production: August 1930 to
August 1932
Price New: £230

Featured Car

Registration Number:
L ???5
Licensing Authority:
Livingstone, Northern
Rhodesia
Registration Date:
1931
Notes: Including this car,
two have been recorded and
neither survives. The sales
brochure states that this
Scorpion model differed
from the others by having a
specially tuned engine, but
it does not describe these
modifications.

These photographs were taken in Livingstone, Northern Rhodesia (the 'L' registration stands for Livingstone). The proud owner standing by the Triumph is my father who worked in the Colonial Service. My parents worked in Northern Rhodesia but were married in Cape Town in February 1937 and then sailed to the United Kingdom for their honeymoon. It was standard practice in those days when working for the Colonial Service to combine a honeymoon with long leave as their employment terms were typically 2½ to 3 years duty followed by 6 months leave.

It was probably shortly after landing in the United Kingdom for their honeymoon that my father bought this Triumph and at the end of their break took it back to Africa with them. Father certainly did this at least twice after the war when he bought a Daimler (possibly a DB14) and a Standard Vanguard.

Another possibility, since my mother is not pictured in these photographs, is that my father bought this Triumph on an earlier leave in circa 1934 and that the right-hand photograph represents the newly exported car in pristine condition and the other later photo shows it battered by the African roads. Before the war there were not many fully tarred roads in Rhodesia. One common solution on 'main' roads was two parallel strips of tar about 15 inches wide and dirt on either side. Over time these strips became raised and driving on and off them became very hazardous, but at least these roads were useable in the wet season.

My father joined the forces shortly after the start of the war and I imagine his Triumph was sold at that time.

Sadly I hardly knew my father and until recently I assumed that his little Triumph was a Super Seven, but I now know (thanks to the Pre-1940 Triumph Owners Club) that it was a much rarer six-cylinder Scorpion.

Stuart Rangeley-Wilson, Norfolk

Specification

Engine: 11.85 hp;
6 cylinders; 56.5 mm bore
by 80 mm stroke; capacity
1,203 cc; side valves; single
carburettor.
Gearbox: 3 forward speeds
and reverse.
Brakes: Lockheed
hydraulically operated on all
four wheels; transmission
handbrake.
Track: 3 ft. 7½ in.
Wheelbase: 7 ft. 8¼ in.
Production: September
1931 to August 1932
Price New: £185

Featured Car

Registration Number:
KJ 991
Licensing Authority:
Kent
Registration Date:
1932
Notes: Including this car,
five have been recorded and
none are thought to survive.
A de Luxe model, produced
from September 1930 to
August 1932, was also
available, initially priced at
£194. For the extra money
the de Luxe came with a
four speed gearbox, leather
upholstery and spring gaiters
as standard fitments.

I purchased this car from Eltisley Garage for £25 in 1954. The car was subject to a court order allowing the garage owner to sell it to recover a debt incurred by the car's owner.

I drove the car home and garaged it at the Wheatsheaf public house in Castle Street, Cambridge. I was under age to drive it legally so I took this opportunity to work on the engine. I fitted oil control rings to the pistons, had the big ends re-metalled and bought a new starter ring which was fitted by Moores of Histon Road, Cambridge. Other engine parts were supplied by Dan Morley Garage of Castle Street, Cambridge. Unfortunately all this work on the car's engine made no noticeable difference to the performance. I was not keen on the two-tone brown bodywork, so I repainted it British Racing Green with black wings.

Sharing the garage at the Wheatsheaf was Derek Stubbings who was building an MG special. On one occasion when we were both working on our cars Derek had a visit from racing driver Archie Scott Brown and Mr Lister whose company built Archie's Lister Jaguar racing car. I remember them looking at my rare Scorpion with interest.

I passed my driving test three weeks after my 17th birthday. I insured the car with Eagle Star at a cost of £13 and bought its road tax for £3 8s. 9d. – all on an apprentice carpenter's wage of £3 a week. The first trip in the car was to Clacton with three of us in the front and two in the dickey seat! Unfortunately for the two 'outside' passengers it rained all the way home and by the time we had reached Halstead the windscreen wiper had stopped working.

The first photograph shows me at the wheel of my Scorpion and my friends Roger Silk, in the passenger seat, and Peter Barber standing next to me. Roger is behind the wheel in the other photograph.

Apart from three occasions when the dynamo burnt-out, each time the result of a misbehaving control box, the car gave me reliable motoring. I had the car for about 18 months before exchanging it for a 1935 Riley Monaco, registered AVE 78, at Reynolds Garage in Castle Street. I received £25 for the Scorpion and paid £125 for the Riley. I saw the Scorpion around Cambridge a couple of times after exchanging it and I think a couple of students had bought it.

David Clark, Cambridgeshire

SUPER EIGHT PILLARLESS COACHBUILT SALOON

Specification

Engine: 7.9 hp; 4 cylinders; 56.5 mm bore by 83 mm stroke: capacity 832.24 cc; side valves; single 'self-starting' carburettor.
Gearbox: 3 or 4 forward speeds and reverse.
Brakes: Lockheed hydraulically operated on all four wheels; transmission handbrake.
Track: 3 ft. 7½ in.
Wheelbase: 6 ft. 9 in.
Production: August 1932 to July 1934
Price New: £155

Featured Car

Registration Number: JW 2585
Licensing Authority: Wolverhampton
Registration Date: January 1933
Notes: Super Eights replaced the Super Sevens and were mechanically, including the chassis, identical to the last specification Super Sevens. 114 Super Eight Pillarless Saloons have been recorded and eight survive with their original style bodywork. This car still exists.

I first saw this car in 1951 when I was about ten years old. It was being driven past our gate by the girl next door to and from her place of work. She lived with her parents in an old farmhouse surrounded by old barns. The car was garaged in one of these barns which it shared with other local cars.

About six years later it had been replaced by her husband's 'modern' car. While 'exploring' I found the little Triumph residing in the corner of one of the barns. I made my interest in the car known and I was subsequently allowed to service it, following which I drove it precisely one mile accompanied by clouds of blue smoke. This is when I took this photograph during 1957 in 'The Big Yard', next to our house, where Parks Department tractors, trailers, gang mowers and other grass maintenance machinery were stored and where I learnt to drive.

About two years later I found that parts had been removed from the Triumph. Wishing to restore it before it suffered further deterioration I was given the car by the owner, 'the girl next door'. While a friend was helping me with work on the car, he unfortunately broke the pistons. I was so disappointed that I put the car in my mother's garage and left it there, only transferring it to my garage after she died. It is still in my garage and recently my son urged me to either sell or restore it. Happily we have started the restoration, but still require new pistons!

Thomas Wells, Gloucestershire

Specification

Engine: 7.9 hp; 4 cylinders; 56.5 mm bore by 83 mm stroke: capacity 832.24 cc; side valves; single 'self-starting' carburettor.

Gearbox: 3 or 4 forward speeds and reverse.

Brakes: Lockheed hydraulically operated on all four wheels; transmission handbrake.

Track: 3 ft. 7½ in.

Wheelbase: 6 ft. 9 in.

Production: August 1932 to July 1934

Price New: £155

Featured Car

Registration Number: JY 1679

Licensing Authority: Plymouth

Registration Date: Mid 1933

Notes: Super Eight saloons were offered only in 'Pillarless' form. With the front and rear doors open the pillarless design allowed for unobstructed access in and out of the car. They can be distinguished from Super Sevens by their different style radiator surround, Magna wheels and the standard fitment of bumpers. This car no longer exists.

SUPER EIGHT PILLARLESS COACHBUILT SALOON

My earliest memories starring the Triumph were of camping trips to Scotland during the post-war years 1948 to 1950. This small car contained two adults in the front, three children aged between four and 13 years squashed in the back along with one boisterous dog, plus assorted camping equipment and luggage either in the boot or strapped to the luggage rack. Our job as children was to take turns in checking that nothing had fallen off the back.

My mother always recorded a journal of our holidays and one such recording of a Saturday in July 1948 relates to a special trip to the 'Sadlers' in Banchory, Scotland, to purchase a new fan belt costing 2/6d.

The following is a shortened extract from Mam's journal recording the journey from our home on Teesside to Banchory:

Scotland. July 8th 1949. Left home at 7.12 am, mileometer reading 37,468. Five gallons of petrol. Route A177. Stockton at 7.30 am. Durham at 8.12 am. Route A1. Newcastle at 8.53 am, milometer reading 37,512. Morpeth at 9.30 am, milometer reading 37,525. stopped for ten minutes for a snack. Belford at 11.00 am, milometer reading 37,569. Berwick at 11.20 am, milometer reading 37,574. Stopped for dinner at 12.45 pm. Left at 1.00 pm. Stopped for four gallons of petrol, milometer reading 37,621. Edinburgh at 1.45 pm, milometer reading 37,630. Queensferry, on at 2.30 pm, off 2.50 pm. A90 Route. Kinross at 3.35 pm, milometer reading 37,656. A94 Route. Milometer reading 37,668. Perth at 4.15 pm, milometer reading 37,673. Stopped for tea and left at 5.10 pm. Stonehaven at 7.25 pm, milometer reading 37,741. Banchory at 8.20 pm, milometer reading 37758. 290 miles travelled from leaving home.

The Triumph was used for three years for our annual trip to Scotland followed in subsequent years by trips to London. It was eventually replaced by a Wolseley saloon car more suited to a growing family.

John Taylor, Middlesbrough

SUPER EIGHT PILLARLESS COACHBUILT SALOON

Specification

Engine: 7.9 hp; 4 cylinders; 56.5 mm bore by 83 mm stroke: capacity 832.24 cc; side valves; single 'self-starting' carburettor.
Gearbox: 4 forward speeds and reverse.
Brakes: Lockheed hydraulically operated on all four wheels; transmission handbrake.
Track: 3 ft. 7½ in.
Wheelbase: 6 ft. 9 in.
Production: August 1932 to July 1934
Price New: £175

Featured Car

Registration Number: BMF 899
Licensing Authority: Middlesex
Registration Date: 1934
Notes: During the final year of production these Super Eights received small styling changes. These included four sets of louvres on the bonnet sides (similar to the newly introduced Gloria models) and raised body mouldings at waist level. Only one of these later style Super Eights survives. This car no longer exists.

My father and brother bought 'old jalopy' as it was affectionately known (photographed above with my father, mother and myself) in 1955 for £28 10s. I was a very disappointed seven year old because earlier the same evening they had brought home a beautiful streamlined silver Alvis which needed rewiring. It was priced at £45 which they had decided was far too expensive and had settled for this old black workhorse instead. At least it was a car! Few of my working class contemporaries could boast a family car and we only had one because my father had learned to drive in the Army during the war. He was now working as a six-ton van driver who could see the social potential of motoring and my brother was determined to learn to drive so he could visit home at weekends from national service at RAF Waddington. We all cheered when it almost touched 50 mph downhill on the outward journey of one of its first outings with four adults and me aboard but disgraced itself the same evening when it broke down with six miles to go for home in the city of London. It actually broke down quite a lot and gave us a particularly embarrassing Saturday afternoon when it broke a half shaft and held up all the traffic at the Staples Corner junction of London's busy (even then) North Circular Road.

In the first summer it was used for the family holiday to Ramsgate and generally gave a good account of itself but my brother managed to fail the first of two driving tests, never quite getting on terms with either the car's juddery clutch or my father's bad temper when he got things wrong. We always had to be careful to properly close the doors as the upper latch on the handle levers often failed to fully locate and with the pillarless design of the body the doors were only held shut by the single pin at the bottom.

The car was lacking power and was clearly approaching the end of its 22 year career. Hills were becoming a problem. One day with my mother and aunty on board (both ladies of reasonable proportion) the old jalopy got halfway up East Heath Hill in Hampstead and ground to a stop. A kind gentleman who was walking doffed his trilby and opened the door for the two fat ladies to get out. We never did find out if the man was aware of the shortcomings of the car, but I will never forget the hysterical laughter of the embarrassed sisters as they clambered back in at the top of the hill.

As autumn 1956 closed in the demise of 'old jalopy' was as certain as the bad weather to come. On a foggy Saturday morning the scrap man came and our first car was gone. So what for 1957? Well we couldn't exist without a motor so we invested in a really modern 1938 Austin 12!

John Sharp, Berkshire

Specification

Engine: 8.9 hp; 4 cylinders; 60 mm bore by 90 mm stroke; capacity 1,018 cc; overhead inlet and side exhaust valve; single Solex self-starting carburettor.
Gearbox: 4 forward speeds and reverse.
Brakes: Lockheed hydraulically operated on all four wheels; transmission handbrake.
Track: 3 ft. 7½ in.
Wheelbase: 7 ft. 8 in.
Production: September 1931 to August 1933
Price New: £185

Featured Car

Registration Number:
Unknown
Licensing Authority:
Unknown
Registration Date:
Unknown
Notes: The Super Nine was the first Triumph to be fitted with the Coventry Climax designed overhead inlet/side exhaust valve engine. 115 Super Nine Saloons have been recorded and 14 still survive with their original bodywork. This car is not thought to be one of the survivors.

SUPER NINE 6-LIGHT COACHBUILT SALOON

My father, Francis Jefford Hartland, bought this Super Nine soon after his return from working in Canada in 1933. He married my mother in March 1934 and I believe he had this little car then and retained it until he bought a Fiat Topolino in either 1936 or 1937.

This photograph of my father with the car was taken in the Haslemere area possibly at nearby Hindhead.

In later times I recall that he always spoke well of it with special mention of the hydraulic brakes. Possibly influenced by his ownership of this car he bought another Triumph in the 1950s, this time a Gloria (see page 31).

Richard Hartland, Hampshire

SUPER NINE 6-LIGHT COACHBUILT SALOON

These photographs of my father's Triumph were taken with his 'Box Brownie' camera in 1934 on the B852 road which runs alongside Loch Ness in Scotland. They were posed so as to appear to be looking for the 'monster'! My grandfather retired in 1934 and this was celebrated by taking a touring holiday in Scotland. My father, Jack, drove and the other passenger was my Aunt Marjorie, his sister. My grandparents were John and Edith Day.

My father bought the Triumph new following the sale of his two-seater Swift. I believe my grandfather never drove as the Triumph would have been better suited for my father to drive my grandparents about, now they had moved from Leytonstone, Essex, to a house they had built in Saltwood, Kent (*this house can be seen on page 4*).

Unfortunately I do not know what happened to the Triumph. My father must have sold it prior to 1940 because during the Second World War he owned an Austin Seven.

Paul Day, Hertfordshire

Specification

Engine: 8.9 hp; 4 cylinders; 60 mm bore by 90 mm stroke; capacity 1,018 cc; overhead inlet and side exhaust valve; single Solex self-starting carburettor.
Gearbox: 4 forward speeds and reverse.
Brakes: Lockheed hydraulically operated on all four wheels; transmission handbrake.
Track: 3 ft. 7½ in.
Wheelbase: 7 ft. 8 in.
Production: September 1931 to August 1933
Price New: £185

Featured Car

Registration Number: AEV 257
Licensing Authority: Essex
Registration Date: March 1933
Notes: In August 1932 these saloons received slightly revised bodywork with re-styled front wings. This car no longer exists.

Specification

Engine: 8.9 hp; 4 cylinders; 60 mm bore by 90 mm stroke; capacity 1,018 cc; overhead inlet and side exhaust valve; single Solex self-starting carburettor.
Gearbox: 4 forward speeds and reverse.
Brakes: Lockheed hydraulically operated on all four wheels; transmission handbrake.
Track: 3 ft. 7½ in.
Wheelbase: 7 ft. 8 in.
Production: September 1931 to August 1933
Price New: Unknown

Featured Car

Registration Number: OW 1770
Licensing Authority: Southampton
Registration Date: 1932
Notes: The club has records for Super Seven, Super Eight and Scorpion Tickford Sunshine Saloons. This is the only Super Nine version to be recorded and no literature relating to this model has been seen. This car no longer exists.

The left-hand photograph was taken when the Triumph was practically new and before my ownership. The crowd of people are looking at the damage following its collision with a motorcycle combination during a morning rush hour in 1932.

My friend Norman and I bought this beige and black car in early 1939 in Ealing, West London, for £26. It replaced our Triumph Super Seven which we had owned for a year and cost £13 to buy.

We seemed to have more sunny days then so the roof was often open (as can be seen in the right-hand photograph with Norman and Geoff, who also shared digs with us) and with petrol at 1/6d a gallon we made many trips around the country at weekends. Rather than look for accommodation whilst out and about during those weekends, at night we would slide out the front seats, put the back seat on the floor and with pillows and cushions made it comfortable enough to sleep in the car. Lowering and raising the fabric roof was made simple by inserting a winding handle at the rear side of the bodywork.

After being called up in September 1939 (I was in the S.R. Royal Signals) the car was sold to a farmer in Yorkshire, but I cannot remember exactly where.

Unfortunately during the last few weeks of our ownership we had trouble. One of the cylinders had worn and the plug had to be cleaned fairly regularly, but that was the only problem we ever had with this car. It served us well.

I am now 93 years old (as at May 2008), a member of the Institute of Advanced Motorists and now drive a Vauxhall 1.4-litre Corsa. Since selling the Triumph in 1939, I have never seen, nor come across reference to another exactly the same. When I contacted the Pre-1940 Triumph Owners Club to find out more about this model I was surprised when they showed me photos of my car when it was less than a year old and further surprised to see it had been in an accident, but now looking closely at my photo the offside front wheel does look as though its got more negative camber than it should have! I understand that these photos were only recently sent to the club by Tim Harding (a motoring photograph/postcard collector and author).

Geoffrey Clark, Oxfordshire

SUPER NINE 4-SEATER TOURER

These photographs were taken in 1952 and show my dad Clifford, mother Elsie and myself with our Triumph. Dad bought it just after marrying mother in 1945. Dad was born in 1921 and started work as an apprentice gardener, then worked at the Earldom Brickworks in Whiteparish near Salisbury (my wife, Mary, and I still occupy this site with our haulage company). The brickworks closed at the start of the war and re-opened later as a sawmill. It was at the brickworks where the Triumph was first registered.

The Triumph was painted blue with brown interior and was powered by a Coventry Climax engine, which dad had reconditioned in the early 1950s. It was bought from United Services Garage (Portsmouth) Ltd. I know that because I still have the badge somewhere that was taken off the dashboard. As kids, we used to go on trips to Torquay in it, which is about 120 miles away. There was a folding luggage rack on the back near the spare wheel on which dad used to put the picnic basket.

In those days you were able to tax cars for three months at a time so dad, who could not afford the road tax for a full year, only taxed it for six months. It was kept in the garage for the other six months. He was very fussy about keeping things right and looking after them. Dad eventually sold his Triumph in 1957.

In the late 1970s I had the privilege to see dad's old Triumph, amongst old racing cars, in a private museum in Norfolk and remember telling the chap in charge that I was not pleased that it was now painted green instead of the original blue! Since then I am happy to report that it has now been beautifully restored back to its original colour scheme and is in good hands.

Brian Snelgar, Wiltshire

Specification

Engine: 8.9 hp; 4 cylinders; 60 mm bore by 90 mm stroke; capacity 1,018 cc; overhead inlet and side exhaust valve; single Solex self-starting carburettor.
Gearbox: 4 forward speeds and reverse.
Brakes: Lockheed hydraulically operated on all four wheels; transmission handbrake.
Track: 3 ft. 7½ in.
Wheelbase: 7 ft. 8 in.
Production: September 1932 to August 1933
Price New: £198

Featured Car

Registration Number: RV 3691
Licensing Authority: Portsmouth
Registration Date: June 1933
Notes: This is one of only two examples that the club has recorded. Both survive in excellent condition. This car featured on page 24 in the first book, which covers its ownership by Charles James from 1960 to the mid 1970s.

Specification

Engine: 9.8 hp; 4 cylinders; 63 mm bore by 90 mm stroke; capacity 1,122 cc; overhead inlet valves; single carburettor.

Gearbox: 4 forward speeds and reverse.

Brakes: Lockheed hydraulically operated on all four wheels; transmission handbrake.

Track: 3 ft. 7½ in.

Wheelbase: 7 ft. 8 in.

Production: September 1932 to August 1933

Price New: £225

Featured Car

Registration Number: NG 24-95

Licensing Authority: Holland

Registration Date: June 1934

Notes: Not long after their introduction the engine capacity was increased from 1018 cc. and the 'Nine' was dropped from the Southern Cross Nine Tourer model name. 12 of these Southern Crosses (both engine sizes) have been recorded and six are thought to survive.
This car exists in excellent restored condition.

SOUTHERN CROSS TOURER

It was in August 1961 that I fell in love with this Southern Cross when it was for sale in a second-hand car lot. Even though it was in poor condition I bought the car and started a low budget restoration, which was all I could afford being a student at the time. The restoration took me three years to complete.

Meta, my future wife, and I decided that we would use the newly finished car for our camping holiday to Belgium. We could not holiday this way in Holland as in those days unmarried couples were not allowed to camp together on Dutch campsites – even though I was 30 years old! Soon after we arrived on the campsite the car's distributor developed a problem. Before long many campers had gathered to watch my attempts to repair it and with the help from an assortment of parts they had gathered together I had the car running again. The first photograph shows me tackling another small repair during this holiday on the same campsite.

Our journey home from Belgium turned into disaster when the engine sprung an oil leak from the rear crankshaft bearing into the gearbox bell housing. This slowed our progress home as every ten miles or so we were forced to make a stop to place a tin under the gearbox to collect some of the leaked oil. We then put it back in the engine along with some new oil. After the 150 mile journey we had used over two gallons of oil and our top speed for the last few miles was only 25 mph!

I dismantled the engine, renewed the bearing, and rebuilt it just in time for our wedding on 7th July 1965 as can be seen in the second photograph.

All too soon the engine started leaking oil again via the same rear crankshaft bearing. Rather than sell the Triumph I decided to store it until I was in a position to undertake a high quality restoration. It was not until 1984 that we started its restoration when my son Martyn prompted me to do something about the 'old car' that had always sat in our barn. By 2001 we had finished the rebuild and drove the Triumph over to England for the Pre-1940 Triumph Owners Club's annual rally. I was pleased that it was well received and was proud to be awarded with a trophy during their prize giving.

Martin Smitt, Holland

SOUTHERN CROSS TOURER

Specification

Engine: 9.8 hp; 4 cylinders; 63 mm bore by 90 mm stroke; capacity 1,122 cc; overhead inlet valves; single carburettor.
Gearbox: 4 forward speeds and reverse.
Brakes: Lockheed hydraulically operated on all four wheels; transmission handbrake.
Track: 3 ft. 9 in.
Wheelbase: 7 ft. 8½ in.
Production: September 1932 to August 1933
Price New: £225

Featured Car

Registration Number: OC 698
Licensing Authority: Birmingham
Registration Date: 1933
Notes: This, the second of three Southern Cross Tourer models, received slight modifications to its chassis, bodywork and fittings. 27 have been recorded and eight survive. This car no longer exists.

I owned this Triumph between 1952 and 1953 when I was in the Navy. These photographs were taken outside my home in Rochester, Kent.

A friend of mine Roy Clark, a builder by trade from Strood in Kent, was a keen car restorer and I often helped him with his cars. In 1952 he bought this Triumph and completely stripped it down and rebuilt it in a year with my help. When it was finished I was surprised and pleased when Roy asked me if I would like to buy it for £150. The deal was done and I spent a further £15 on having a hood and side screens made.

My first real run in the Triumph was returning to my naval base at Bodmin in January 1953. There was deep snow everywhere which made overnight driving fun! The only trouble encountered was that the brakes would lock on when applying them too hard down the Devon hills. I took the Triumph to a local garage where the brakes were bled. This cured the problem.

Home on leave I left the Triumph in a local car park overnight and to prevent the engine from freezing I placed a camel hair coat over it. When I returned to the car park for an early morning return to Bodmin the car was gone. I contacted the police and by 10.00 am they had found it abandoned in Dartford. I later discovered that three boys had escaped from borstal that night and taken my Triumph as their getaway car. Roy and I towed it back home to Strood with his car as the engine had seized. This was due to a lack of water when a buckle from the coat had hit and holed the radiator. I returned to Bodmin by train and a fortnight later I had a phone call from Roy to say that I could collect the car, which I did with pleasure. Roy had rebuilt the engine and only charged me for the oil! It is great to have friends.

The Triumph served me well in Cornwall and Devon. Every weekend I and several friends would go somewhere regardless of the weather with complete reliability and a fair turn of speed.

I eventually exchanged the Triumph for a 1950 Kingford Special owned by Peter Proctor who was a great motoring enthusiast at the Bodmin base. I think that the Triumph ended its life against a brick wall after narrowly missing an elderly lady!

Eric Wooddin, Surrey

Joan Margaret Richmond

Born in Cooma, N.S.W., Australia in 1905 Joan became one of the most successful lady drivers in motor sport during the 1930s, with much of her success driving Triumphs. Before her driving exploits she tried horse racing but in the mid-1920s women jockeys were not accepted so she entered motor sport making her name in Australian hillclimbs, trials and races. Joan was based in Britain in the early 1930s when driving Rileys. Other cars she drove in the 1930s included MG, Fiat, HRG and Delage.

Following the tragic death of her fiancé, Bill Bilney, during wet conditions in a motor race at Donington. Joan stayed in Britain until 1946 when she returned to Australia. With little money or sponsorship for motor racing she concentrated her efforts on animal welfare.

Joan died, aged 94, on 11th August 1999 and on the Richmond family gravestone it reads: 'Racing Motorist and Animal Lover'.

The photographs are reproduced courtesy of David Price (1st & 4th), Tim Harding (2nd) and Derry Aust (3rd).

COMPETITION SPECIAL

In 1933, Triumph's Colonel Holbrook engaged my aunt, Joan Richmond (pictured above left), as a driver in the work's competition team and in this role she competed in numerous UK and Continental events, using the little Southern Cross two-seaters and often partnered by her close friend Eva Gordon Simpson (pictured above right with Joan).

Joan said that Holbrook believed success in competition would sell cars but this policy was not fruitful and eventually the works team was disbanded. However, Holbrook persuaded his fellow directors to allow the company to continue supporting those owners that wished to use their cars in competition.

Most of the team cars were sold off but some of the most competitive cars were 'sold' to the drivers. That is how Joan became the owner of KV 6904, one of the two specials that Donald Healey had built for the 1934 Monte Carlo Rally. No money changed hands, but officially it became her car and the registration was transferred accordingly. However it was still looked after by the factory mechanics, an arrangement that suited Joan admirably. Most of the works cars were painted pale green but as she had not had much success with them she had KV 6904 painted red with yellow wheels.

Joan said: "It was a lovely car, wonderful to drive, although initially it didn't have enough weight on the front wheels for racing. Donald had put the engine a bit too far back in the chassis so that when you were doing 100 miles an hour down the straight at Donington it didn't behave very well. Lord Howe, who was acting as an observer when I tested her, put it rather well, saying that it was one of the most dangerous cars he had ever seen at Donington and that 'it only tapped its front wheels on the ground occasionally'. I must say that was exactly what it felt like. We cured the problem by getting hold of an extra large battery and installing it in the space between the engine and the radiator."

"The engine was a very special 1232 cc Coventry Climax with a Laystall crankshaft that would rev to 6,000 rpm without any trouble, which was pretty high in those days. I'm sure even the engine block was made of something special, everything seemed to be different from the standard engine. It could also be run supercharged when necessary with a large Centric blower, similar to that fitted earlier in the year to Jack Ridley's successful Monte Carlo Rally car. With big powerful brakes, a large radiator and a powerful clutch, it was a very competitive car."

"I first drove this car in competition at Donington in August 1935, supercharged on this occasion, finishing second in a five lap handicap and third in the later five lap championship race. A few days later I won the Ladies' Trophy in the Singer Car Club open trial, which was a pretty good start."

COMPETITION SPECIAL (continued)

Specification

Engine: 4 cylinders; 66 mm bore by 90 mm stroke; capacity 1,232 cc; overhead inlet and side exhaust valve; probably fitted with twin carburettors when not supercharged.
Gearbox: 4 forward speeds and reverse.
Brakes: Lockheed hydraulically operated on all four wheels.
Track: Unknown
Wheelbase: Unknown
Production: December 1933
Price New: Not listed

Featured Car

Registration Number: KV 6904
Licensing Authority: Coventry
Registration Date: December 1933
Notes: This car was last licensed for the road on 19th June 1961 and its sister car KV 6905 had a much shorter life being last licensed on 17th July 1935. Neither of these cars survive.

"With the support of the Triumph competition department, I entered my car for the 1936 Monte Carlo Rally and as I wanted to score as many points as possible I selected Umea in Sweden as my starting point, rather a chilly spot in midwinter as it is only about 100 miles south of the Arctic Circle. My co-driver was to be Geoff Brooks, one of the young men that drove regularly in the rallies that we entered and who I thought would back me up very well. Geoff was also good fun, having a good sense of humour which I liked."

When the time came to disembark from Tilbury to Gothenburg, they were seen off by various friends including Joan's fiancé Bill Bilney and her mother. Joan said she was a bad sailor and didn't like sea travel so she headed straight for her cabin and bed. Geoff, on the other hand, got talking with Archie Scott, a tall, shy fellow who was the only other British competitor on board. It seemed that Archie, an ex-Guards officer and now a society bookmaker, whom they had seen at previous events, told Geoff that he hadn't spoken to them on previous occasions because he imagined that professional drivers wouldn't want to know him.

As Archie had been there before, the next morning he guided them in his Bentley out of the Gothenburg docks and the two cars then ran together at a very fast pace to Stockholm for an overnight stop. Their arrival in Sweden being dependent on the ship, they spent a few days in Umea before the start of the Rally having various madcap midwinter adventures in which Archie was a willing participant. They had all become firm friends. Just as well, for along the road sometime later they found Archie had slid off the road and was stuck nose first in a snowdrift. So they pulled him out and pressed on to Monte Carlo where they finished 20th. Zamfirescu was the winner, starting from Athens in a Ford. Donald Healey was 8th in the rebuilt Dolomite. Archie finished a respectable 45th out of only 72 finishers.

To quote Joan: "We finished in 20th position, and what's more we tied for second place in the 1500 cc class which delighted us enormously. The light car class winner was Kozma, in a Fiat, who started from Tallinn. He got more points than we did on the road and although the Triumph performed marvellously in the special tests, making fastest time in the class, we just couldn't make up the deficit. Geoff (above photographed leaning on KV 6904 in Paris during this event) had been a marvellous co-driver. If you had confidence in your co-driver you could, even in a little car like the Triumph, curl up and go to sleep so that you were reasonably fresh when it was your turn to drive. I think this was my best performance in a Monte Carlo Rally."

The right-hand photograph shows Joan sitting in KV 6904 proudly displaying the trophies they won together.

David Price, Australia

Specification

Engine: 9.8 hp; 4 cylinders; 63 mm bore by 90 mm stroke; capacity 1,122 cc; overhead inlet and side exhaust valve; single 'easy start' down-draught carburettor.

Gearbox: 4 forward speeds and reverse.

Brakes: Lockheed hydraulically operated on all four wheels with transmission handbrake.

Track: 3 ft. 9 in.

Wheelbase: 8 ft.

Production: March 1933 to August 1933

Price New: £225

Featured Car

Registration Number: UD 6303

Licensing Authority: Oxfordshire

Registration Date: Late 1934

Notes: This is the first of two similar body styles during their 1½ year production run. 106 saloons have been recorded and two survive with their original style bodywork. One is in such poor condition that it is only suitable for spares. This car no longer exists.

TEN SALOON

This is the car in which my father, Jack Jenkins, taught me to drive in 1946 when I was 17. He and my mother, Elsie, are pictured here with me beside him, not long after he bought the royal blue and black car in 1935.

He and my mother had moved from Birmingham when they bought a drapery and hardware shop in Walsall, which was part of a housing estate built during the early 1930s. Previously my mother had been in the rag trade and my father had operated a capstan lathe during the depression following the First World War. For several years after buying the shop my father augmented their income working as a foreman in the plating shop of my uncle's chromium plating factory (Cooper, Webb, Jones and Co.). My father was in the early stages of rheumatoid arthritis and it was wonderful when, instead of having to cycle the two or three miles to work he was able to commute in style driving his Triumph.

I remember the excitement of my father buying this, his first car, at a time when not many people could afford such a luxury. I particularly remember, as I always had to sit in the back, that if someone sat beside me, my half of the seat would noticeably rise.

During the war years petrol rationing curtailed our expeditions in the Triumph but I remember several holidays in Wales and on two occasions (1937/8) we toured Devon and Cornwall in six days. It also took us to the Norfolk Broads for a boating holiday in 1947 and I remember my father proudly saying he had driven 200 miles home on the last day. During the war we managed a week's holiday in nearby Stratford-upon-Avon when I was allowed to take a friend, having no siblings to keep me company.

On precious Thursday afternoons or Sundays, the only time the shop was closed, we would go for day trips to Stratford-upon-Avon, the Cotswolds, Leamington Spa and other interesting places within reach. My mother was very proud of her blue picnic case with its blue and white cups, saucers, plates, knives, forks, spoons, and its tin boxes for sandwiches.

My mother's pride in the car knew no bounds. She regularly cleaned it (my father was restricted by his arthritis) and would admonish him for driving through muddy puddles or too near hedges which might scratch the paintwork. She always dusted the car before washing it (so the dust wouldn't scratch) and after polishing the paintwork would take the chrome hub caps into the house to polish on the (suitably protected) dining table. When, eventually, the car was exchanged in 1948 for an Austin A40 Devon model, my mother was slightly perturbed because the lower roof caused the windows to sit lower and she said "won't people be able to see right inside the car?". I suggested net curtains!

Betty Spanswick, Somerset

23

TEN "POPULAR" SALOON

My husband Ted bought this car before we were married in 1954 and I have no idea what he paid for it. He resprayed it in a lovely shiny black. This photograph was taken on a holiday to Scotland with our friends Betty and Reg Wiley in 1952. Reg can just be seen behind the car and I am sitting on the front bumper (just look at those dreadful trousers!). We had a great holiday and did not have any problems with the car which had travelled many miles by the time we returned home to Wembley.

Soon after our Scottish holiday we decided to sell the car and Reg was keen to buy it. A deal was done and Betty thinks that Ted was paid £112 for the car (this seems a lot to me, but maybe she is right). When Reg drove it home something on the car collapsed! It was repaired but Betty cannot remember how long they kept it.

My brother Pete Tucker is in the car trade and he reminded me that in the 1950s he had many Triumphs through his hands, including Super Sevens, Glorias, Vitesses and Dolomites. He took a liking to a black Dolomite Roadster which he drove for some time. He said that these pre-war Triumphs were good sellers.

Audrey Saunders, Middlesex

Specification

Engine: 9.53 hp; 4 cylinders; 62 mm bore by 90 mm stroke; capacity 1,087 cc; overhead inlet and side exhaust valve; single Solex self-starting carburettor.
Gearbox: 4 forward speeds and reverse.
Brakes: Lockheed hydraulically operated on all four wheels with transmission handbrake.
Track: 3 ft. 9 in.
Wheelbase: 8 ft.
Production: August 1933 to July 1934
Price New: £198

Featured Car

Registration Number: AXE 1?
Licensing Authority: London
Registration Date: December 1933
Notes: This car features the revised bodywork where front and rear doors are rear hinged. On the early style body the front doors were front hinged and the rear doors were rear hinged. No Tens with this later type bodywork survives.

Specification

Engine: 9.53 hp;
4 cylinders; 62 mm bore by
90 mm stroke; capacity
1,087 cc; overhead inlet and
side exhaust valve; single
Solex self-starting
carburettor.
Gearbox: 4 forward speeds
and reverse with free-wheel
pre-selection.
Brakes: Lockheed
hydraulically operated on all
four wheels with
transmission handbrake.
Track: 3 ft. 9 in.
Wheelbase: 8 ft.
Production: August 1933 to
July 1934
Price New: £225

Featured Car

Registration Number:
CYY 58
Licensing Authority:
London
Registration Date: July or
August 1936 when imported
from Jersey
Notes: Compared with the
Ten "Popular" this model
was fitted with a free-wheel
gearbox as standard and also
had opening rear side
windows. None survive.

TEN SALOON

My father, Eric, bought this Triumph when he was working in Jersey during the mid-1930s. He brought it back to mainland Britain in 1936 when the car was re-registered. It was garaged for the duration of the war and then father used it for a short time before it was laid up again.

After I had passed my driving test I persuaded father to let me have the car, as by then he had bought a Morris Minor. I was able to restore it back to running condition, as I was then an apprentice at Lucas. The car's features that I recall were the Coventry Climax engine, free-wheel gear changing, auto starting and those enormous headlamps.

I remember a lot of sweat being emitted when replacing the kingpins and bushes. The worst disaster was discovering that the engine block had cracked between two bores in the water jacket. After much saving, I was put in touch with a firm of specialist engineers who were able to 'cold stitch' it together. While the engine was apart I took the opportunity to have the bores honed, fitted new pistons etc., in short a proper engine overhaul.

Having put the car into decent running order the next task was to restore brake performance. I was fortunate that the local Lockheed distributor employed a school chum of mine who sourced all I needed at staff discount prices. The only two problems that I never cured were oil seeping into the footwell from the gear shift and the Lucas Startix misbehaving.

The photo of Margaret, my fiancée (now my wife), and myself was taken in either 1959 or 1960 on the North Wales coast, possibly at Colwyn Bay. Margaret reminded me of an occasion when we had taken her grandmother out for a drive and she had especially requested that we drove over the Berwyn range to Llangollen. No problem thought I in my youthful foolishness, but a rude awakening came when the car refused a particularly steep ascent incorporating a tight bend in the single track 'road'! It resulted in disembarking the passengers, followed by an ignominious reverse to a point where we had to return from whence we came. It was accompanied by much muttering from the aged relative about young drivers!

Eventually the car had to go, as my apprentice wages were not sufficient to keep it running once I was engaged. After selling it in Wrexham I never saw or heard of it again.

Alan Greaves, Wrexham

GLORIA TEN SALOON

Pictured next to their grey Gloria are Liley, Joan and Jack Shipman, my nan, mum and grandad. These photographs were taken whilst holidaying around 1947. The right-hand photograph shows my grandad with his Gloria and caravan, both proudly owned and especially since he had built the caravan himself. He was a policeman in the Metropolitan Police Force and purchased his Gloria in the late 1930s and sold it circa 1954.

To celebrate nan and grandad's silver wedding in 1946, they embarked on a touring holiday of Britain with my mum and her best friend, Marjorie, in the Gloria. Starting from their home in Bedfont, Middlesex, they travelled up through central England, North Wales, the Lake District and up to Scotland. I still have the family photos of this holiday and they include shots of the Highland Games in Braemar. Their last night of the holiday was spent in Berwick-upon-Tweed on the Scottish border. Mum told me that she bought their silver wedding anniversary present in Berwick. The next day grandad drove from Berwick to Bedfont. He would have driven down the old A1 through all the towns and villages when it was a single lane road. I know there wasn't the high level of traffic then, but having experienced this journey in a modern car on modern dual carriageways, by-passing the towns and villages, I think that it was one heck of a drive!

Grandad ran a youth club when he retired in 1960, after he and nan moved to Barnstaple in Devon. He got on very well with young people and was a super grandad to my sister, Carol, and I. Nan died in 1970 and grandad in 1972; he never recovered from losing her.

Hazel Jenkins, Northumberland

Specification

Engine: 9.53 hp; 4 cylinders; 62 mm bore by 90 mm stroke; capacity 1,087 cc; overhead inlet and side exhaust valve; single 'easy start' down-draught carburettor.
Gearbox: 4 forward speeds and reverse with free-wheel pre-selection.
Brakes: Lockheed hydraulically operated on all four wheels; handbrake operating on rear drums.
Track: 4 ft.
Wheelbase: 9 ft.
Production: September 1933 to August 1934
Price New: £285

Featured Car

Registration Number: AMT 565
Licensing Authority: Middlesex
Registration Date: October or November 1933
Notes: This Gloria was first recorded by the club in the early 1960s when a Mr B. T. Instone from Slough owned it. The bumpers on this Gloria are not a Triumph fitment.
This car no longer exists.

Specification

Engine: 9.53 hp;
4 cylinders; 62 mm bore by
90 mm stroke; capacity
1,087 cc; overhead inlet and
side exhaust valve; single
'easy start' down-draught
carburettor.
Gearbox: 4 forward speeds
and reverse with free-wheel
pre-selection.
Brakes: Lockheed
hydraulically operated on all
four wheels; handbrake
operating on rear drums.
Track: 4 ft.
Wheelbase: 9 ft.
Production: September
1933 to August 1934
Price New: £285

Featured Car

Registration Number:
AUV 461
Licensing Authority:
London
Registration Date:
October or November 1933
Notes: 151 of these Glorias
have been recorded and 13
survive with their original
style bodywork (these
figures include the very
similar Gloria Ten Special
Saloons).

This car no longer exists.

GLORIA TEN SALOON

This Gloria was my father's first motor car and my mother and father are standing proudly next to it in the left-hand photograph. He purchased it in the late 1940s and it would then have been about fifteen years old. The car was used to transport the family including Laddie our dog, who can be seen sitting next to my mother in the right-hand photograph. One of our longest journeys was an overnight drive from London to Holyhead in North Wales. Father would lay-up the Gloria on blocks for the winter. Even though spared the winter conditions it was not the most reliable of cars as it would often stop with a splutter due to a blocked carburettor jet. Roadside maintenance from father was required in order to continue our journey.

On more than one occasion the Gloria's chassis cracked necessitating the attention from a welder's torch. The body colour cannot be recalled but father did give it a fresh coat of paint using a few tins of Brushing Belco.

I can remember as a very young child sitting in the Gloria's rear seat and viewing through the flat windscreen a couple of rows of polished studs on top of the bonnet. These protected the paintwork when the bonnet was folded up from either side of the car.

After quite a few years of ownership father part exchanged the Gloria for a Ford Anglia at Browns Garage in Loughton, Essex. The garage still exists today but I doubt that the Gloria does.

Adrian Dawn, London

GLORIA TEN SALOON

Specification

Engine: 9.53 hp; 4 cylinders; 62 mm bore by 90 mm stroke; capacity 1,087 cc; overhead inlet and side exhaust valve; single 'easy start' down-draught carburettor.
Gearbox: 4 forward speeds and reverse with free-wheel pre-selection.
Brakes: Lockheed hydraulically operated on all four wheels; handbrake operating on rear drums.
Track: 4 ft.
Wheelbase: 9 ft.
Production: September 1933 to August 1934
Price New: £285

It was during 1969 when, whilst still at technical college I found and bought my first car. In those days a car for under a hundred quid usually meant a well used Morris 1000, Austin A35, Ford Anglia or something a little older with a bit more style. My Saturday morning job at a local Doncaster garage introduced me to a Triumph 'Gloria' saloon which stood dusty and unloved in the old car 'graveyard'. In the glove box was a photo that I took home and studied. I'd never been interested in older cars but this was intriguing, had lovely lines and features which I just adored. £75 bought it and she came home literally under her own steam. After some loving care, some light 'restoration' and a few parts it was back on the road. An £8 comprehensive insurance policy and I was away and it was so much better than the Lambretta!
Work and marriage followed and Gloria lay untouched for many years but eventually, in 1993, I grasped the nettle and she got the full nut and bolt restoration she deserved.

Of course, I still have her plus two other Glorias that I have acquired on the way.

Steve Jacobs, Yorkshire

Featured Car

Registration Number: YG 5408
Licensing Authority: Yorkshire, West Riding
Registration Date: November 1933
Notes: Glorias manufactured in the first two months of production had their windscreen wipers mounted at the top of the windscreen frame, as with this car. The wipers were then mounted below the windscreen frame on the bodywork. This car exists in excellent restored condition.

Specification

Engine: 9.53 hp;
4 cylinders; 62 mm bore by
90 mm stroke; capacity
1,087 cc; overhead inlet and
side exhaust valve; single
'easy start' down-draught
carburettor.
Gearbox: 4 forward speeds
and reverse with free-wheel
pre-selection.
Brakes: Lockheed
hydraulically operated on all
four wheels; handbrake
operating on rear drums.
Track: 4 ft.
Wheelbase: 9 ft.
Production: September
1933 to August 1934
Price New: £285

Featured Car

Registration Number:
AXE 20
Licensing Authority:
London
Registration Date:
December 1933
Notes: These Glorias were
not fitted with bumpers as
standard. The front bumper
fitted to this Gloria might be
the type that Triumph
offered as an extra.
This car no longer exists.

GLORIA TEN SALOON

In 1956 we bought our first family car. It was this Gloria pictured above and we paid £20 for it which was all we could afford especially now that we had a daughter. It was painted black with lovely green leather upholstery and blow-up seat cushions. My husband and I both drove the Gloria. I learnt to drive while in the RAF and my husband while in the Army where he trained as a mechanic. This proved useful in looking after and repairing the car. We were fortunate that kindly neighbours allowed us to park Gloria in their lean-to which kept it off the street and sheltered from the bad weather.

We travelled many hundreds of miles in the car including visiting our friends on the Norfolk coast four times a year. It was during these trips that we took these photographs. The one on the left was taken at Cromer and the other during a family picnic at Sheringham featuring my mother, her old friend, myself and daughter Avis (aged two).

The only mishap I can remember having with Gloria was when I was about to drive to hospital to visit Avis. I pulled the choke control right out of the dashboard and with a yard of unattached wire cable on my lap I found it difficult to start the engine! I can also remember that there was some rot in the floorboards which from some angles allowed a good view of the road beneath. In 1958 we moved house and the car had to sit outside unprotected from the weather and during that winter the clutch seized solid – sadly it was time to sell Gloria.

We had a lovely time with Gloria and I cannot recall seeing many others like her at the time but a friend did own a similar larger model. I thought that I would never see another but by chance, in 2005, I heard that there would be a nearby meeting of Pre-war Triumphs at Stanford Hall. I went along in the hope of seeing a Gloria and was not disappointed as there were many on display including one similar to ours. That is when the happy memories came flooding back.

Gwendoline Allen, Leicestershire

GLORIA TEN SALOON

My late father had driven a Gloria in the late 1930s so when he saw this one in 1957 he bought it for the use of my two older brothers and me. It was painted in a striking bright red with black roof and wings.

We were taken with the advance features for a car built in 1934. The large Lockheed hydraulic brakes, 12 inch drums as I recall, looked the part behind the centre lock wire wheels. We thought that they worked well until father and I were checking the adjustment one day and found the rear ones were not working at all apart from the handbrake. The flexible hose to the rear axle was totally blocked with gunge! A new hose and thorough bleeding of the system had the brakes working really well.

When leaving the car parked the master switch, located near the rear seat, was a useful security item. One weak point on the Coventry Climax designed engine was the oil pump which was not up to the job in hot weather, so with the freewheel engaged it gave the engine some respite when going downhill.

I took the Gloria to Crimond aerodrome, near Peterhead, to marshal at one of their very early race meetings. I was able to drive the car round the track to my assigned post. The car was regarded by some as an old jalopy, but it proved to brake and handle a darned sight better than some of the new small Fords!

One of my brothers took the Gloria to Edinburgh for the summer term at university. At the end of term he enjoyed the drive home, via the ferry over the Forth, and reached home somewhat sooner than usual!

It was decided to sell the Gloria so, following comments about the bright 'fire engine red' body, father and I obtained the use of a large garage and repainted the whole car using Valspar black paint and good quality brushes. We had the car for about two years, but I do not recollect who bought it from father.

This photograph was taken on 13th May 1958 on the Kinmundy Road, Peterhead.

Ian Douglas, Perthshire

Specification

Engine: 9.53 hp; 4 cylinders; 62 mm bore by 90 mm stroke; capacity 1,087 cc; overhead inlet and side exhaust valve; single 'easy start' down-draught carburettor.
Gearbox: 4 forward speeds and reverse with free-wheel pre-selection.
Brakes: Lockheed hydraulically operated on all four wheels; handbrake operating on rear drums.
Track: 4 ft.
Wheelbase: 9 ft.
Production: September 1933 to August 1934
Price New: £285

Featured Car

Registration Number: HH 7481
Licensing Authority: Carlisle
Registration Date: Mid 1934
Notes: This car no longer exists.

Specification

Engine: 9.53 hp;
4 cylinders; 62 mm bore by
90 mm stroke; capacity
1,087 cc; overhead inlet and
side exhaust valve; twin
'easy start' down-draught
carburettors.
Gearbox: 4 forward speeds
and reverse with free-wheel
pre-selection.
Brakes: Lockheed
hydraulically operated on all
four wheels; handbrake
operating on rear drums.
Track: 4 ft.
Wheelbase: 9 ft.
Production: September
1933 to August 1934
Price New: £300

Featured Car

Registration Number:
AXC 520
Licensing Authority:
London
Registration Date:
November 1933
Notes: In addition to the
twin carburettors, other
features that distinguished
these cars from the
'standard' Ten Saloon were
a high lift camshaft,
polished ports and a
different style dashboard to
include a rev-counter.
This car no longer exists.

GLORIA TEN SPECIAL SALOON

Photographed with his second Triumph (*see page 15 for details of his first*) is my father Francis and our two Cocker Spaniels, Sally and Jilly, on the drive of our house in Greyshott near Hindhead. It was taken in either 1953 or 1954 by me, aged about 15, and with help from my friend Gordon Madgwick who also owned a Triumph (*see page 51*) I developed the film and printed this photograph myself.

The Gloria was painted black over apple green with green leather upholstery. The engine had lost its twin carburettor set-up and had been replaced by a single side draught S.U. carburettor which I understand from current owners of these Glorias would not have produced any noticeable downturn in performance.

Richard Hartland, Hampshire

GLORIA TEN SALOON

I bought this car in Broadmeadow (Newcastle, New South Wales) in 1956 from an air force chap at the Williamtown air base. This photograph shows me with the car. It was in good sound condition and the only damage was a repaired rear aluminium mudguard with a piece added using aircraft rivets!

At the time I was at teachers college in Newcastle and my home was in Muswellbrook so I regularly drove it between the two places.

My first teaching post was at Captain's Flat in January 1958 and this entailed a long drive from Muswellbrook via Canberra and the Gloria didn't miss a beat. Altogether I did the return trip three or four times without any trouble.

Teaching at Captain's Flat entailed a weekly visit to Braidwood. I travelled about 30 miles on a rough dirt road over the Great Dividing Range and headed north-eastwards to Braidwood. I used to urge the Gloria to go faster on this length of road, and on one trip spun it on a sandy stretch! Another time I had just reached Braidwood when I lost the steering due to a ball joint popping off. It was quite easy to fix and this was the only real problem I had with the car in two years of ownership.

Motoring in the car was enjoyable and although the suspension was firm, the leather front seats were good. The freewheel was a useful feature and it returned an excellent petrol consumption of 34-35 mpg. The rough dirt roads used to shake the dashboard loose and I had to have the wiring loom secured behind it.

I traded it in to a garage in Captain's Flat (they were an agent for Burke's Motors in Cooma, second-hand car dealers) for £150, and after two weeks the son of a mining engineer working at Lake George Mines bought it. Would you believe he took the perfectly good body off it and mechanically stripped the car for the chassis? Such was the car's fate.

John Daniel, Australia

Specification

Engine: 9.53 hp; 4 cylinders; 62 mm bore by 90 mm stroke; capacity 1,087 cc; overhead inlet and side exhaust valve; single 'easy start' down-draught carburettor.
Gearbox: 4 forward speeds and reverse with free-wheel pre-selection.
Brakes: Lockheed hydraulically operated on all four wheels; handbrake operating on rear drums.
Track: 4 ft.
Wheelbase: 9 ft.
Production: September 1933 to 1935
Price New: In the region of £445 Australian

Featured Car

Registration Number: AA 425
Licensing Authority: New South Wales, Australia
Registration Date: 1934
Notes: In 1933 and 1934 Triumph exported Glorias to Australia as rolling chassis to be bodied by local coachbuilders. This Gloria was completed by Ruskin Body Works in Melbourne. This car no longer exists.

Specification

Engine: 9.53 hp;
4 cylinders; 62 mm bore by
90 mm stroke; capacity
1,087 cc; overhead inlet and
side exhaust valve; single
'easy start' down-draught
carburettor.
Gearbox: 4 forward speeds
and reverse with free-wheel
pre-selection.
Brakes: Lockheed
hydraulically operated on all
four wheels; handbrake
operating on rear drums.
Track: 4 ft.
Wheelbase: 9 ft.
Production: September
1933 to 1935
Price New: £445 to £465
Australian

Featured Car

Registration Number:
AYS 858
Licensing Authority:
New South Wales, Australia
Registration Date:
1934
Notes: This Gloria was
bodied by Cresswells in
Melbourne. It is thought
that it was first owned by
Mary, wife of the aviator Sir
Charles Kingsford Smith,
who also owned an identical
Gloria.
This car no longer exists.

GLORIA TEN SALOON

In 1957 I was 17 and doing my engineer training at the BMG Quarry at Prospect, west of Sydney. I rode my bike the seven miles to work each day, and to college about four evenings a week.

I wanted a car and set my heart on an Austin Seven Meteor. The only one I found was £80 but I had only saved £50. At weekends in 1958 I hunted in the second hand car yards along Parramatta Road. On one occasion I saw the same car arriving at different yards. Obviously the owner was trying to trade his car for something else. I eventually asked the owner if he wanted to sell. He said "yes" and wanted £50. The car was a 1934 Triumph Gloria in a light green colour with an iridescent finish. It was long, low with big headlights flanking the extensive bonnet. My desire for an Austin Seven just disappeared.

The owner drove his car to my home in nearby Merrylands where my dad gave his approval. I parted with my money and started enjoying the delights of owning what would prove to be a classic.

It had a few minor problems that we put right and I drove the car daily to work and to the University of NSW at Kensington. For its age the Triumph was remarkably reliable once I discovered the secret of maintaining the SU fuel pump.

For some silly reason I resprayed the car grey. A bad choice, as I now feel that I should have retained the original colour. My friends with other makes of cars envied my hydraulic brakes. They always provided confidence in stopping no matter what the conditions and were technically advanced compared to the brakes fitted to other cars years younger than the Triumph.

I discovered that Arthur Wood, one of the maintenance employees at the quarry, also owned a Gloria. Not only that, he also owned a Triumph Southern Cross Sports Tourer that he drove to work every day. Obviously we became good friends and shared knowledge and experiences with our Triumphs.

After a couple of years I traded the Gloria for a 1952 Holden. I have lots of fond memories of my first car and the enjoyable times I had with my mates as I thrashed around the countryside in my Gloria. My selective memory has suppressed the niggling difficulties that seemed a way of life with cars in those days.

Dennis Percival, Australia

GLORIA SIX SALOON

Specification

Engine: 12.95 hp;
6 cylinders; 59 mm bore by
90 mm stroke; capacity
1,476 cc; overhead inlet and
side exhaust valve; single
'easy start' down-draught
carburettors.
Gearbox: 4 forward speeds
and reverse with free-wheel
pre-selection.
Brakes: Lockheed
hydraulically operated on all
four wheels; handbrake
operating on rear drums.
Track: 4 ft.
Wheelbase: 9 ft. $8^{1}/_{16}$ in.
Production: September
1933 to August 1934
Price New: £325

This is my black and cream Gloria which I purchased in 1957 for £28. I owned it for a couple of years while I was in the RAF. I remember it with great affection, being beautifully made it was quiet on the road. It did however have one minor fault – it ran a big end every 300 miles or so. Father, a hotelier in Bromsgrove, and I devised a system whereby after fitting a new big end the engine would be well enough to get me back to camp (Empire Test Pilot School, Boscombe Down) and return home before having to fit another one. Therefore on each return journey the sump would be removed and the con rod taken into Birmingham to be re-metalled. Father or one of the hotel staff would be dispatched on Friday afternoon to collect this repaired piece of metal (I seem to remember it cost 10s) and when I arrived home I would lie under the car, usually in filthy weather, to fit the offending part.

Eventually I grew tired of this ritual and sold the car to a Vulcan pilot for £65 and spent the next few months trying to avoid him! To replace the Gloria, I managed to find another quality car, made in Coventry, a Riley Kestrel, which served me well for the next year or so.

Trevor Morgan, Warwickshire

Featured Car

Registration Number:
JE 645
Licensing Authority:
Isle of Ely
Registration Date:
1934
Notes: 64 have been
recorded and it is estimated
that three survive with their
original bodywork (these
figures include the very
similar Gloria Six Special
Saloon).
This car no longer exists.

GLORIA SIX SALOON

These photographs show my father sitting first on the wing and then running board along with his housekeeper and his friend. They were on a visit to Bovey Tracey on the edge of Dartmoor in Devon.

We lived in the remote village of Rusper, about five miles from anywhere, and because of the continual battering the Gloria received from country lanes the wheels had to go to a local engineering works to have the spokes replaced. Father ran The Wayside Garage in Rusper near Horsham in Sussex and the Gloria was specifically used for going out on breakdowns and some taxi work. During the war petrol was rationed and our petrol pumps where taken over by local army units encamped outside the village so Gloria probably never came back into her own until after the war.

I did my national service from 1947 to the end of 1949. After demob I joined a choral society in the next village and Gloria was needed once a week to get me there. Driving back one evening, after singing my heart out, I was aware of a continuous ringing from the car behind – it was a police car. In those days they had a small church type bell with an electric 'dinger'. On stopping, the policeman informed me that the Gloria's rear number plate light was out and on inspection we realised it had been squashed flat! Someone had reversed the Gloria into something solid. The policeman asked if had I far to go. I said: "No, just to the next garage". He then told me to drive carefully and carry on.

Happy motoring times, especially with Gloria.

Antony Brooking, Sussex

GLORIA SIX SPECIAL SALOON

In January 1956 I started a new job as a mechanic working for Reg Day Motor Services at Hanwell, London, W.7. In their yard was this Triumph, its engine was out, having been rebored and the crankshaft ground ready for reassembly. After asking I was told that the Gloria had been bought by Peter Hinton Motors, Southall, in 1954 and had been taken to Reg for repair. The engine was seized and the camshaft was beyond repair and it took two years to find a replacement. Peter Hinton eventually gave the Gloria to Reg to cover the cost of his mechanical work.

I found the Gloria interesting and suggested that we assemble the engine and get it running as a spare job when we were not busy. After three months we had it running and I soon wanted to buy the Gloria. Reg sold it to me for £110 including £10 towards a respray in British Racing Green, its original colour had been 'French Grey'.

After its 'running in' period I drove the Gloria to Dickens and Jose, West Ealing, to have the carburettors checked and tuned, this cost £3.14s.

The Gloria initially had problems with the petrol feed but this was cured after having the tank cleaned and tin plated. With new brake cylinder seals, new batteries and five replacement window glasses, the originals had gone yellow, we were back on the road.

It was a lovely car to drive with excellent brakes, steering and road holding. These photos were taken on a Sunday afternoon in 1957 at the top of West Wycombe by the local landmark called the 'Church with the Golden Ball'. They show me fiddling with something under the dashboard and my girlfriend, Beryl, 'posing' on the Gloria's front wing. Behind the Gloria my friend's MG TB can just be seen.

I sold the Gloria in 1958 for £125 after I had driven about 20,000 miles in her. Its new owner lived in West Sussex.

Brian Parkes, Buckinghamshire

Specification

Engine: 12.95 hp; 6 cylinders; 59 mm bore by 90 mm stroke; capacity 1,476 cc; overhead inlet and side exhaust valve; twin 'easy start' down-draught carburettors.
Gearbox: 4 forward speeds and reverse with free-wheel pre-selection.
Brakes: Lockheed hydraulically operated on all four wheels; handbrake operating on rear drums.
Track: 4 ft.
Wheelbase: 9 ft. 8$^{1}/_{16}$ in.
Production: September 1933 to August 1934
Price New: £340

Featured Car

Registration Number: AXY 180
Licensing Authority: London
Registration Date: February 1934
Notes: In addition to the twin carburettors, other features that distinguished these cars from the 'standard' Six Saloon were a high lift camshaft, polished ports and a different style dashboard to include a rev-counter.
This car no longer exists.

Specification

Engine: 12.95 hp;
6 cylinders; 59 mm bore by
90 mm stroke; capacity
1,476 cc; overhead inlet and
side exhaust valve; twin
'easy start' down-draught
carburettors.
Gearbox: 4 forward speeds
and reverse with free-wheel
pre-selection.
Brakes: Lockheed
hydraulically operated on all
four wheels; handbrake
operating on rear drums.
Track: 4 ft.
Wheelbase: 9 ft. 8¹/₁₆ in.
Production: September
1933 to August 1934
Price New: £340

Featured Car

Registration Number:
RD 5382
Licensing Authority:
Reading
Registration Date:
1934
Notes: This car no longer
exists.

In 1961 we lived in a flat near Henley, during which time we replied to a local advert offering a Triumph Gloria for sale, something always difficult to resist! On asking about the Gloria's history we were told the father of the family had driven the car from the factory when new and that some heavy timber had distorted the body while stored. We found no direct evidence of this and as the body and mechanics seemed in excellent condition we decided to buy the Gloria. It cost us £27 10 shillings.

The colour was red and black with 18 inch wheels and inflatable seats. The engine was fitted with two down-draught Zenith carburettors and an inlet manifold designed by a committee and certainly not by an engineer! The engine ran perfectly and the free-wheel was a help considering the performance of its early type clutch which was renowned for juddering.

One unfortunate attribute, discovered early on, was a tendency for the rear doors to fly open often when driving over bumps in the road! This was alarming with babies on the back seat so we resorted to tying the doors together with a length of string.

Another quite exciting experience took place at the lights at Mere Corner, south of Warrington, near Liverpool, on a wet night. On applying the brakes, the car made a 90 degree turn without changing direction. With rapid right-hand lock applied things corrected themselves and no harm was done except to our nerves. The old hardened tyres may have contributed to this episode.

The left-hand photograph shows Jackie and the children picnicking at Binfield Heath near Henley-on-Thames. The other photo was taken on the shore at Ainsdale, between Southport and Liverpool. It was not quite so crowded then.

We sold Gloria to a local chap in the autumn of 1961.

Frank & Jackie Jones, Hampshire

GLORIA MONTE CARLO TOURER

This Monte Carlo was owned by my friend John Bauley from the north west London area. We served our apprenticeships together at the de Havilland Engine Company and studied at university together.

I have many memories of John and his Monte Carlo. The one that stands out was when we were on our way back to university, driving up the A1 to Newcastle at night in the depth of a winter blizzard. I was ahead in my Morris Minor and John was following in his Monte Carlo. Somewhere near Catterick I saw John's headlights spin around and then disappear. On turning back I found John with the car in the ditch. Totally unworried he said "You carry on to the hall of residence and put the kettle on, I expect a lorry will come past soon and pull me out!" Forty minutes after my arrival at Newcastle there was John!

After graduation in 1958 we were joined by our friend, Alan Warriner, for a continental tour in the Monte Carlo of France, Belgium, Germany, Luxembourg, Switzerland and Italy. These photographs were taken on this tour above the snow line in the Alps, with the left-hand photograph showing our luggage and tent strapped to the front wings and on the petrol tank by the spare wheels. Happy days!

Alan White, Dorset

Specification

Engine: 10.8 hp; 4 cylinders; 66 mm bore by 90 mm stroke; capacity 1,232 cc; overhead inlet and side exhaust valve; twin 'easy start' down-draught carburettors.
Gearbox: 4 forward speeds and reverse with free-wheel pre-selection.
Brakes: Lockheed hydraulically operated on all four wheels; handbrake operating on rear drums.
Track: 4 ft.
Wheelbase: 9 ft.
Production: January 1934 to August 1934
Price New: £325

Featured Car

Registration Number: KV 9614
Licensing Authority: Coventry
Registration Date: August 1934
Notes: 25 have been recorded and 13 still survive with their original style bodywork.
This car still exists in excellent condition.

Specification

Engine: 10.8 hp;
4 cylinders; 66 mm bore by
90 mm stroke; capacity
1,232 cc; overhead inlet and
side exhaust valve; twin
'easy start' down-draught
carburettors.
Gearbox: 4 forward speeds
and reverse with free-wheel
pre-selection.
Brakes: Lockheed
hydraulically operated on all
four wheels; handbrake
operating on rear drums.
Track: 4 ft.
Wheelbase: 9 ft.
Production: January 1934
to August 1934
Price New: £325

Featured Car

Registration Number:
AYW 750
Licensing Authority:
London
Registration Date: 1934
Notes: Before Laurence's
ownership this car was
driven by John Baldwin (a
motoring journalist for *The
Motor*) when he followed
and reported on the 1934
Alpine Rally. The car was
lent to him by Newnhams,
Triumph's main London
agent.
This car no longer exists.

GLORIA MONTE CARLO TOURER

I purchased this green Monte Carlo in 1937 with 40,000 miles on the clock. In July of that year a friend and I decided that for our holiday we would take the car to the Arctic Circle and back. This we did in just under 13 days by catching a boat from Harwich to Esbjerg in Denmark, driving up through Sweden to Norway (where the first photograph was taken), back into Sweden to Finland and then onto the Arctic Circle. While in Sweden on our way to Finland we suffered our only mishap. We hit a two foot boulder which bent a front spring and wing but luckily these were repaired locally for only eight shillings! On the return leg we travelled down through Finland to Turku where we caught a boat to Stockholm, drove to Denmark and then shipped back to England. The car performed remarkably well on the variable road conditions and considering that we drove it hard for 3,133 miles we were pleased to average 27 mpg.

The following year three friends and I took the car to Val d'Isère where we enjoyed some high-altitude skiing (the second photograph shows me with the car and skis). Following torrential rain, our road in the Haute Savoie was partially washed away and blocked by a rock fall. Local labour managed to create a narrow strip through the debris and a small post van cautiously bumped its way across. Then I drove across with one car following before the whole lot avalanched away! The road was closed for two days.

Before and during the war, based in London and afterwards in Scotland, I was involved in the supply of oxygen therapy equipment to hospitals so the car served as auxiliary transport in the emergency service. With the front passenger seat and rear seat cushion removed three large oxygen cylinders, a complete oxygen tent, icebox and a one hundredweight block of ice could be carried!

The car's charmed life was much in evidence during the London blitz. On the way home during the night of the 'City Fire Raid' I was stopped near Marble Arch by a 'fire assessor' who asked if I could get him as near to the fire area as possible. We tailed a fire engine part of the way. When we approached Fleet Street the road was littered with incendiaries (some still burning) but we managed to pick our way through to Ludgate Hill where my passenger left me. I will never forget the awesome, but majestic, sight of St Paul's floodlit by blazing buildings. On the way back the car was violently accelerated down a street by a bomb blast – thankfully it did not fall in front. On another night I drove into an unmarked large hole full of debris and managed to bump and scramble out unscathed. Retracing the route a little later I found that the road was closed and guarded with a circle of dim red lights around the hole. Asking why the road was closed when, shortly before, I had driven through the hole and all from the opposite direction, I was told that this 'large hole' was the shallow crater of an unexploded bomb and that I was the lucky one as I must have driven right over it!

The car had become an integral part of my life and it was a sad day when I exchanged the Monte Carlo in the early 1950s for the car of my dreams (*see page 114*).

Laurence Hole, Hertfordshire

GLORIA MONTE CARLO TOURER

Specification

Engine: 10.8 hp; 4 cylinders; 66 mm bore by 90 mm stroke; capacity 1,232 cc; overhead inlet and side exhaust valve; twin 'easy start' down-draught carburettors.
Gearbox: 4 forward speeds and reverse with free-wheel pre-selection.
Brakes: Lockheed hydraulically operated on all four wheels; handbrake operating on rear drums.
Track: 4 ft.
Wheelbase: 9 ft.
Production: January 1934 to August 1934
Price New: £325

Featured Car

Registration Number: BUL 65
Licensing Authority: London
Registration Date: January 1935
Notes: The smaller 1,087 cc engine could be ordered for this model. The club has recorded two with this engine option.
This car still exists in excellent condition.

'Ferdie' as our Gloria became known cost David, my father, £180 from Weeks scrapyard at Instow near Barnstaple in 1952, when he was at Dartmouth Naval College. It became a much better investment than the naval uniform that he should have been buying!

David made a few changes to the car such as making brackets to support Koni dampers to replace the worn out original type. He also removed the built-in jacks to reduce weight. The car was unusual in having front wings with an added vertical panel welded on to follow the profile of the wheel, as opposed to the original more open design. Ferdie was used as my parents' 'going away' car for their wedding in 1955, as can be seen in the first photograph.

In 1958 Ferdie took my parents and my older sister, Penelope (only ten months old at the time), faultlessly on a seven week continental tour. This included going over the Alps from Switzerland into Italy towing a trailer loaded with their camping gear.

In the early 1960s we travelled through a blizzard up a steep hill and passed stranded vehicles. Ferdie kept moving due to its tall skinny tyres cutting through the snow. Those were the days before there was lots of traffic and no seat belts, with Ferdie often loaded with our parents, four children in the back and our meagre luggage on a carrier over the spare wheels! The second photograph was taken in April 1960 and features family members and their 'vehicles'.

We moved to Canada in 1967 when David was seconded to the Canadian Navy for two years. Ferdie was carefully laid up in my grandmother's garage with corrosion inhibiting oil in the engine and a thick layer of wax over the chrome work.

We bought a Peugeot 404 Estate in Canada and when we returned it came back with us. With father being frequently at sea it didn't make sense to return Ferdie to roadworthy condition. Every time we went to see our grandmother the first thing I would ask to see was the car. I loved to remove a little of the wax and see the chrome gleaming! Something I feel a bit guilty about now. I really hoped Father would get the car back on the road one day. My wish came true when in 2001 he handed Ferdie over to A. C. Royle & Co Ltd. near Darlington to be restored and they did a magnificent job.

Father kept Ferdie until his death in 2004, aged 72. In 2008 our family reluctantly decided to sell Ferdie as we felt that we were not in a position to keep it in the superb condition that father had achieved. It now has a new owner who hopefully will continue to enjoy the car as our family did.

Nick Atkins, Somerset

Specification

Engine: 10.8 hp;
4 cylinders; 66 mm bore by
90 mm stroke; capacity
1,232 cc; overhead inlet and
side exhaust valve; single
S.U. carburettor.
Gearbox: 4 forward speeds
and reverse with free-wheel
pre-selection.
Brakes: Lockheed
hydraulically operated on all
four wheels; handbrake
operating on rear drums.
Track: 4 ft. 2 in.
Wheelbase: 9 ft.
Production: September
1934 to August 1935
Price New: £298.

Featured Car

Registration Number:
BNA 280
Licensing Authority:
Manchester
Registration Date:
January 1935
Notes: 119 have been
recorded and 11 survive
with their original style
bodywork.
This car no longer exists.

GLORIA SALOON

I purchased my grey Gloria in June 1951 when I returned from doing national service in the Suez Canal zone in Egypt. The car was purchased from a Mr Papworth who was an Inspector at Crewe Police Headquarters. It was christened 'Penelope' by all the family who enjoyed nine years of happy motoring with her. These photographs were taken in the mid 1950s. In the first, I can just be seen leaning out of the side window and in the other Barbara, my wife, is posing with Penelope in a local country lane.

During our time with Penelope I had to do many mechanical and body repairs in my garage at home. There were not many spares available in the 1950s and I can remember having a water manifold made at a local engineering works. To help matters, I purchased another Gloria from London. Luckily I had relatives living at Highgate so they arranged to buy it and have it put on a train to be forwarded to Crewe railway station sidings. When it arrived I towed it from the sidings to my home, near Nantwich, where it stood for a few years. Some spares were used but I found out later that it was not quite the same model as mine. Even so, I kept the engine and gearbox for the next 50 years or so and have only just sold them.

Penelope had blow-up air cushions in the front seats which were really comfortable until they punctured! We would then use a cushion or two from the house until they were repaired. When I engaged the gearbox's free-wheel it was a funny feeling coasting down hills with the engine just ticking over with no control from the gears – most disconcerting. On occasions the engine would stop due to fuel starvation. Through previous experience it meant that I had to jump out of the car, tap the fuel pump with whatever came to hand to coax it back into life, jump back in and off we went again. The final thing that really sticks in my mind is that the body creaked in frosty weather.

Even though it was a lovely car I sold Penelope to a chap near Crewe in about 1960 but I still have my fond memories of her and a few photographs.

Joe Chadwick, Cheshire

GLORIA SALOON

Specification

Engine: 10.8 hp;
4 cylinders; 66 mm bore by
90 mm stroke; capacity
1,232 cc; overhead inlet and
side exhaust valves; single
S.U. carburettor.
Gearbox: 4 forward speeds
and reverse with free-wheel
pre-selection.
Brakes: Lockheed
hydraulically operated on all
four wheels; handbrake
operating on rear drums.
Track: 4 ft. 2 in.
Wheelbase: 9 ft.
Production: September
1934 to August 1935
Price New: £298

Featured Car

Registration Number:
Unknown
Licensing Authority:
Unknown
Registration Date:
Unknown
Notes: It is unlikely that
this car still exists.

During the Second World War this Gloria was the workhorse of the photographic section of the Airborne Forces Experimental Establishment that made preparations for the airborne invasion of Europe on D-Day. As you can see by the poor quality of these photographs it is doubtful whether they were taken with one of their official cameras! The Gloria carried a film crew, which included my father, and equipment to dropping zones of paratroopers and gliders. The sunroof was used as a good vantage point to get shots of parachutes landing and the first Jeep to be dropped from the air. This prototype half-Jeep, half-autogyro machine was initially towed to get airborne behind a 4.5-litre supercharged Bentley, but this was not successful. Eventually the Jeep did 'fly' when it was pulled aloft by a Whitley bomber, but it broke up on impact with the ground!

The Gloria was based at AFEE Sherburn in Elmet, Yorkshire, and then at Beaulieu, Hampshire, when the unit moved there in 1945. With petrol on ration the Gloria was modified to run on aviation fuel.

My father also recalled that it was involved in a police chase when someone in the Gloria threw a bottle out of the window on the way back to camp after a night out. The bottle hit a bobby on a bike who gave chase through the New Forest. Fortunately for the Gloria's occupants they got back to the AFEE base, which was a restricted area, before the policeman, saving them a brush with the law!

In the left-hand photo the Gloria's 'blackout' markings can be seen on the edges of the wings and running board together with the headlamp mask. The front bumper has been removed, perhaps with the intent to lighten the Gloria for some extra speed.

Robin Bird, Merseyside

Specification

Engine: 10.8 hp;
4 cylinders; 66 mm bore by
90 mm stroke; capacity
1,232 cc; overhead inlet and
side exhaust valve; single
S.U. carburettor.
Gearbox: 4 forward speeds
and reverse with free-wheel
pre-selection.
Brakes: Lockheed
hydraulically operated on all
four wheels; handbrake
operating on rear drums.
Track: 4 ft. 2 in.
Wheelbase: 9 ft.
Production: September
1934 to August 1935
Price New: £298.

Featured Car

Registration Number:
CS 1566
Licensing Authority:
Ayrshire
Registration Date:
1935
Notes: This car is fitted
with a centre chrome strip
down its radiator grille. This
is not a factory fitting but
amongst the club's many
old photographs it is not
uncommon to see this
feature on other Glorias.
This car no longer exists.

GLORIA SALOON

This photograph picturing the two Triumphs owned by our family was taken by my cousin, Glyn Lancaster Jones, sometime round 1962 at a caravan site at Penrhyn Bay in North Wales. In this photograph are my father, Mervyn Begent, whose sister was Glyn's mother, and a family friend from France who was staying with us.

My father had bought the black Gloria Saloon (on the left) from a colleague at work in the early 1950s as a replacement for the second of two early 1930s Citroën Twelves, remembered as substantial but not very exciting. This Gloria Saloon had really seen better days, but was eminently reliable and much endowed with 'battleship' patches on the mudguards, especially round the headlamp attachments. At one time my father fitted Tufnol bushes to the kingpins. This was fine until one wet morning on the way to work when they became swollen and he found he was unable to turn into the works car park! So it was back to the drawing board.

This Gloria stayed in the family until about 1964 when it was replaced by a similar car in considerably better condition (*see page 71*).

The story for the other Gloria in this photograph also features in this book (*see page 60*).

Roy Begent, Cheshire

GLORIA SALOON

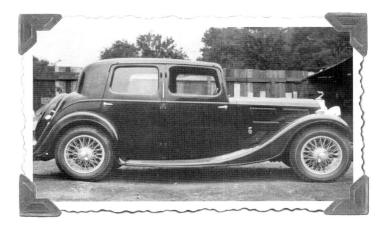

I was born in 1923 and as far back as I can remember my parents always had a car, and I can remember back to 1925!

First we had a Bean, an open car, which I fell out of (quite a frequent occurrence in those days). Then an Essex, a big saloon car, then a Ford Eight (the first car costing only £100) and then, I guess in about 1936, a Triumph Gloria. At this stage we had moved to a farm in the Cotswolds. I was still at a boarding school in Maidenhead so had to be ferried in the Gloria backwards and forwards to school at the beginning and end of terms.

The Triumph was a delightful car, black with a silver mascot on the front (not allowed these days, I gather). My mother called the Gloria Mrs Merdle (*vide* Dickens) because she was so quiet. Her body was made of aluminum, as a young man discovered to his horror when he made the mistake of colliding with her and the repairs were more expensive than a steel bodied car.

The Gloria could be put into neutral, by engaging the free-wheel, so that she could run downhill with just the aid of gravity. Consequently when we reached the slope on the eastern side of the Cotswolds driving over to Maidenhead, the Gloria could be run in neutral for several miles, though my father never dared to drive her in neutral down the steep hill from Bisley to Stroud.

Ruth Hadman, B.Sc., Ph.D., Suffolk

Specification

Engine: 10.8 hp; 4 cylinders; 66 mm bore by 90 mm stroke; capacity 1,232 cc; overhead inlet and side exhaust valves; single S.U. carburettor.
Gearbox: 4 forward speeds and reverse with free-wheel pre-selection.
Brakes: Lockheed hydraulically operated on all four wheels; handbrake operating on rear drums.
Track: 4 ft. 2 in.
Wheelbase: 9 ft.
Production: September 1934 to August 1935
Price New: £298

Featured Car

Registration Number: Unknown
Licensing Authority: Unknown
Registration Date: Unknown
Notes: It is unlikely that this car still exists.

Engine: 15.72 hp;
6 cylinders; 65 mm bore by
100 mm stroke; capacity
1,991 cc; overhead inlet and
side exhaust valves; single
horizontal carburettor.
Gearbox: 4 forward speeds
and reverse with free-wheel
pre-selection.
Brakes: Lockheed
hydraulically operated on all
four wheels; handbrake
operating on rear drums.
Track: 4 ft. 2 in.
Wheelbase: 9 ft. 8¹/₁₆ in.
Production: September
1934 to August 1935
Price New: £350

Featured Car

Registration Number:
BYH 421
Licensing Authority:
London
Registration Date:
June 1935
Notes: This model's body
and fittings are identical to
the four-cylinder version,
apart from the longer
bonnet and front wings. 35
have been recorded and six
survive with their original
style bodywork.
This car no longer exists.

GLORIA SIX SALOON

This Gloria was purchased by my father, Ernie Rickman, who owned and ran a garage in Ashley near New Milton in Hampshire. Unusually, it was fitted with built-in hydraulic jacks on front axle and rear wheels and was operated by a lever under the passenger seat. The Gloria was laid up during the war and left on blocks in the corner of the garage.

When petrol became available again, father reconditioned the car and resprayed it yellow and black (I think that it was originally cream and black). In the 1930s father rode for Southampton Speedway and after the war he purchased a competition bike for off-road use. Unfortunately he died before he could take part. My brother, Don, and I were aged 13 and 15 at this time and our mother, Marjorie, took over the business. She did not discourage us from taking an interest in the bike and allowed us to ride it on the rough ground behind the garage. As soon as we were old enough to gain competition licences we started to ride in events and travelled around the south of England winning scrambles and trials. The Gloria was used to transport the bike to and from the events. This was done by removing the bike's front wheel and bolting its forks to a frame on the Gloria's rear bumper. The driver to all the events at this time was mother. I remember the Gloria being very reliable and we used it to about 1951.

Don and I went on to be successful in the motocross world winning events around Europe. We also became members of the Great Britain motocross team in the 1960s, riding our own Metisse motorcycles developed by ourselves. The right-hand photograph shows us in action.

The Metisse motorcycles became popular and we started production on a commercial basis. Our star customer was Steve McQueen who was a big fan of our bikes and visited our factory to order his machine.

After the motorcycles we then went into kit car production using a galvanised chassis with a fibre-glass body. Over a 1,000 cars were made and many can be seen on the road today. We also developed a sports car before selling the company in 1991.

Derek Rickman, Hampshire

GLORIA SIX SALOON

My father, Sidney Dyas, rebuilt this car (photographed using my mother's 1920s Kodak Box Brownie camera) between 1950 and 1953 for his brother, Edward, who lived in Evesham Street, Redditch. Uncle Edward owned this Gloria from about 1949 to 1954.

The left-hand photograph was taken in August 1951 and shows (from left to right) my father, myself and father's friend Norman Wheal who re-trimmed the car's interior. Norman was a trimmer by trade and worked for the Austin Motor Company at Longbridge. My father and I also worked at Longbridge where I was an apprentice toolmaker from 1951 to 1957 and continued to work there until 1972. Father was an inspector on rear axle assemblies and then on the 'new' engine and gearbox production lines, initially for the Austin A30s, until 1962. He was in the motor trade from 1924 except during the war when he was in charge of Spitfire fuselage assembly at Castle Bromwich.

Our next door neighbour, Charlie Turner, who was a tinsmith by trade and then a panel beater in his later years, repaired and replaced some of the bodywork. Most of this work was done outside and was reliant on the weather. It caused plenty of interest amongst friends and neighbours.

Two things clearly stand out in my mind about the rebuild. The first was helping father cut and shape all the timber frames from the rotten ones at a timber yard at the bottom of our road (their name, Parsons, can just be seen above the restored car in the right-hand photograph take in July 1953). The second was the laborious and time consuming task father gave me of cleaning and preparing the spoked wheels; this took me as long to complete as it did for the rest of the car to be restored! When it became time to apply the final coat of paint to the car we were forced to wait ages for the weather to be just right, but it was worth it.

In July 1953 on the day after my 17th birthday Uncle Edward gave me my first driving lesson in his Gloria and with his guidance I drove from Redditch, Worcestershire, to Stratford-upon-Avon. After that he continued to teach me in and around Redditch and the Cotswold area. I passed my test first time in the following January.

I have fond memories of this car and they were renewed following a chance meeting with two Glorias and their owners whilst staying at a farmhouse during a holiday in the Cotswolds in August 2005.

David Dyas, Dorset

Specification

Engine: 15.72 hp; 6 cylinders; 65 mm bore by 100 mm stroke; capacity 1,991 cc; overhead inlet and side exhaust valves; single horizontal carburettor.
Gearbox: 4 forward speeds and reverse with free-wheel pre-selection.
Brakes: Lockheed hydraulically operated on all four wheels; handbrake operating on rear drums.
Track: 4 ft. 2 in.
Wheelbase: 9 ft. 8$^{1}/_{16}$ in.
Production: September 1934 to August 1935
Price New: £350

Featured Car

Registration Number: BXJ 497
Licensing Authority: Manchester
Registration Date: December 1935
Notes: It is interesting to note that this car was registered four months after production of this model had ceased.
This car no longer exists.

GLORIA VITESSE SALOON

I took this photograph of my friend, Tim Lack, with his Gloria parked behind my father's house in Woking, Surrey, in the early 1960s. Tim arrived one day and proceeded to dismantle it. The happy and relaxed smile is symptomatic of someone who has not fully realised what is wrong with their car! My late father came out to view the chaos outside his garage and after a few minutes turned to me and said "Does he really know what he is doing?" Apparently he did know something of the problem because it eventually disappeared under its own steam.

I remember Tim buying this black Gloria for about £20 from his friend, David Battie, who is now the well known antiques expert appearing regularly on the BBC's *Antiques Roadshow* television programme.

On one occasion when travelling in the Gloria with Tim along Shores Road, Woking, the rear axle started to make a terrible noise. On inspection we found it to be full of rusty water instead of oil! It was refilled with oil and this did quieten it down a bit but it always tended to whine.

At this time I was driving a 1950s German built 400cc Glas Goggomobil. Being typical young lads we were keen to see who had the fastest car, so to find out we raced each other from Maybury towards West Byfleet passing Pryford Common. It was neck and neck all the way with both cars having very similar performance. Luckily there were no other cars on the road, unlike now! My guess is that the Gloria's top speed would have been higher on a long straight road.

I cannot remember when Tim sold his Gloria or what became of it, but he did mention that he had recently seen its BKM 1 registration advertised for sale with the asking price of £26,500!

John Lukey, Surrey

GLORIA VITESSE SALOON

Specification

Engine: 10.8 hp;
4 cylinders; 66 mm bore by
90 mm stroke; capacity
1,232 cc; overhead inlet and
side exhaust valves; twin
S.U. carburettors.
Gearbox: 4 forward speeds
and reverse with free-wheel
pre-selection.
Brakes: Lockheed
hydraulically operated on all
four wheels; handbrake
operating on rear drums.
Track: 4 ft. 2 in.
Wheelbase: 9 ft.
Production: September
1934 to August 1935
Price New: £320

Featured Car

Registration Number:
AAO 931
Licensing Authority:
Cumberland
Registration Date:
November 1934
Notes: Gloria Vitesses were
fitted with a different style
dashboard, to house a large
rev-counter and
speedometer, compared
with the 'standard' Gloria
model.
This car no longer exists.

I owned this car for 18 months between 1953 and 1954, during which time it gave few problems and took me on two long distance holidays. I bought it from a car dealer for about £125.

I was living in Kent at the time and the first holiday with the car was to Edinburgh. I was accompanied by an old school pal who helped with the navigation. He can just be glimpsed sitting in the passenger seat in the right-hand photograph. With so many miles covered during this holiday an engine oil change and fresh lubrication to other moving parts was required before we returned home.

The following year I holidayed in Wales, this time with a different friend. The weather was very wet on our journey there. We soon found that the windscreen was far from watertight and were forced to place a plastic mac over our knees in an attempt to keep our trousers dry! Water was also spouting from around the handbrake lever every time I drove though one of the numerous deep puddles in the road. During the holiday I was very pleased with how well the car coped with the steep Welsh hills.

The Triumph's moment of glory came when I drove the bridesmaids to my cousin's wedding, adorned with the obligatory white ribbons. Soon after I was forced to sell the car, as I would soon be off to work overseas. I found myself with little time to advertise the car, so I sold it for £85 to a different car dealer to the one I had purchased it from.

I was very proud of this Triumph during my ownership and have happy memories.

Peter Tims, Norfolk

Specification

Engine: 10.8 hp;
4 cylinders; 66 mm bore by
90 mm stroke; capacity
1,232 cc; overhead inlet and
side exhaust valves; twin
S.U. carburettors.
Gearbox: 4 forward speeds
and reverse with free-wheel
pre-selection.
Brakes: Lockheed
hydraulically operated on all
four wheels; handbrake
operating on rear drums.
Track: 4 ft. 2 in.
Wheelbase: 9 ft.
Production: September
1934 to August 1935
Price New: £320

Featured Car

Registration Number:
ATV 210
Licensing Authority:
Nottingham
Registration Date:
November 1934
Notes: The external
difference between the
'standard' Gloria and the
Gloria Vitesse saloons was
the lower roof line of the
latter. It is acknowledged
amongst many Triumph
enthusiasts that this and the
six-cylinder version are the
prettiest pre-war Triumph
saloons.
This car no longer exists.

GLORIA VITESSE SALOON

My father's passion for cars started prior to November 1929 when at 16 years old he started an apprenticeship with Armstrong-Siddeley in Coventry.

My brother's first recollection of father's Gloria was seeing it covered up in our garage just after the war. My own first clear memory of Gloria was when I was five years old. We were returning from a family holiday and I was in the front passenger seat. I had reason to turn around and as I did so I must have had my hand on the door handle because the door opened and I flew out. I picked myself up, luckily only suffering from very bad grazes, and started running along crying "Daddy stop!" When I fell out we were travelling at about 50 miles per hour so it took him quite a while to stop. Father told me afterwards that his recollection was one minute I was sitting next to him and then in a flash I was gone. I was very lucky to escape without serious injury. Now I know why they call these rear hinged doors suicide doors!

On the occasions that we went for rides in the Purbeck Hills in Dorset, my brother and I would stand on Gloria's running boards ready to jump off so that we could quickly open and close the many field gates that we would have to pass through. Comparing these times with life today and all its associated health and safety issues, it now appears that we had a dangerous childhood!

Pictured is my mother standing next to Gloria. The photo was taken during 1953 in Poole, Dorset. The car was painted black and red with red leather interior and looks as though the wheel spinners were in need of re-chroming. Mother also drove Gloria – in fact she was a very good driver as she and father drove ambulances in Coventry during the war.

In 1956 while driving to Coventry for a family funeral, father saw a car for sale in a Banbury showroom. It was a Riley Roadster painted racing green with a cream hood. Later that week he part exchanged Gloria for the Riley.

Karen Farrell (née DeRitter), Portugal

GLORIA VITESSE SALOON

Just visible in this treasured and badly faded photograph are my father and his maroon Gloria. According to family lore, father bought this car in 1936 for £120. Father continued to partially use his Gloria during the war as he was fortunate to receive a war work petrol allocation. He edited a journal on the international metal trade. His war work was advising the Ministry of Economic Warfare and the Non-ferrous Metals Control at Rugby, alongside keeping the journal going.

When father first had the Gloria we lived in Ilford and he would regularly rush off with friends and relatives 'to see it do 70' on the Eastern by-pass. He was very pleased to conclude a business trip to Birmingham by getting back to Ilford in two and a half hours (no M1 motorway then).

At the end of the war we had a very low budget holiday in a cottage near the Dorset coast, during which time father happily spent one wet day fashioning a new near-side front floor for the Gloria out of driftwood! Even though my father was proud of his Gloria it had its problems and those arising after the war were aggravated by the complete lack of Triumph spares. For my brother and me the main problem turned out to be a hole in the exhaust which fed fumes into the back seats. This was only discovered when a near-side front spring broke and mother had to squeeze in the back with us behind father to balance the car. It was then that she complained of the smell!

It was the first car I drove, quite illegally, on holiday on Dartmoor aged fifteen. Having changed up through the gearbox I shoved it back into third gear. Father was not pleased! He had been brought up on 'crash' gearboxes and his ability to do a snappy change into bottom gear saved our bacon when travelling up hills on several occasions. In, I guess, 1945 or '46, it developed a badly burnt exhaust valve and was well down on power. The valve was replaced by a mechanic in our garage at home and whilst doing so dropped a collet into the engine, which turned a problem into a crisis! He eventually had to remove the sump where it was found.

Father sold his Gloria in 1947, for the same amount as he had paid, to the Chief Inspector at Redhill Police Station. Its replacement was an Austin A40 Devon.

Trevor Tarring, Surrey

Specification

Engine: 10.8 hp; 4 cylinders; 66 mm bore by 90 mm stroke; capacity 1,232 cc; overhead inlet and side exhaust valves; twin S.U. carburettors.
Gearbox: 4 forward speeds and reverse with free-wheel pre-selection.
Brakes: Lockheed hydraulically operated on all four wheels; handbrake operating on rear drums.
Track: 4 ft. 2 in.
Wheelbase: 9 ft.
Production: September 1934 to August 1935
Price New: £320

Featured Car

Registration Number: BXL 54
Licensing Authority: London
Registration Date: March 1935
Notes: This car no longer exists.

Specification

Engine: 10.8 hp;
4 cylinders; 66 mm bore by
90 mm stroke; capacity
1,232 cc; overhead inlet and
side exhaust valves; twin
S.U. carburettors.
Gearbox: 4 forward speeds
and reverse with free-wheel
pre-selection.
Brakes: Lockheed
hydraulically operated on all
four wheels; handbrake
operating on rear drums.
Track: 4 ft. 2 in.
Wheelbase: 9 ft.
Production: September
1934 to August 1935
Price New: £320

Featured Car

Registration Number:
BXL 103
Licensing Authority:
London
Registration Date:
March 1935
Notes: This is the first of
two coincidences where
owners' memories on the
same car were received.
More can be read about this
Triumph on the next page.
This car no longer exists.

GLORIA VITESSE SALOON

I took these photographs of my Gloria in 1955 beside the A286 (Haslemere to Midhurst road) near the top of Henley Hill. The hill in the background, Blackdown, is the highest in the south of England at 918 feet above sea level.

When I owned this Gloria I also owned and ran a small roadside garage about two miles south of Hindhead on the A3 Portsmouth road. My memories of this car have now faded, however I can remember that I bought it from a Mr Frank Saidder who ran a childrens' home in Hindhead. I improved the Gloria, drove it a little and then sold it on. Unfortunately this is the extent of my memories of this handsome car.

Gordon Madgwick, Hampshire

GLORIA VITESSE SALOON

Specification

Engine: 10.8 hp;
4 cylinders; 66 mm bore by
90 mm stroke; capacity
1,232 cc; overhead inlet and
side exhaust valves; twin
S.U. carburettors.
Gearbox: 4 forward speeds
and reverse with free-wheel
pre-selection.
Brakes: Lockheed
hydraulically operated on all
four wheels; handbrake
operating on rear drums.
Track: 4 ft. 2 in.
Wheelbase: 9 ft.
Production: September
1934 to August 1935
Price New: £320

Featured Car

Registration Number:
BXL 103
Licensing Authority:
London
Registration Date:
March 1935
Notes: This Gloria has been
fitted with 'ACE' wheel
discs. All Glorias were fitted
with centre-lock wire wheels
and these wheel discs were
an optional extra. They
clamped over the wire
wheels, giving the
appearance of solid steel
wheels.
This car no longer exists.

In the late 1950s Dad was very keen on purchasing a Gloria after admiring an example owned by one of his customers with a business in the Birmingham Jewellery Quarter. Dad was 'bitten by the bug' and acquired a Gloria from his friend Harry 'Rag' who worked in a posh Birmingham garage. Business was conducted in the nearby 'Boulton Arms' and for a couple of pints of mild, bread 'n' cheese and £10 the deal was done! The left-hand photograph of Dad with Gloria was taken soon after.

Gloria was kept in a group of warm wooden garages alongside an early Hillman Minx, an Austin A30 and a Ford Prefect. The garages were a meeting point on Saturdays for fathers and sons (this was when my love affair with cars began). The men had nicknames. Wilf 'Crippen' (he looked like him) who worked at Lucas in Great King Street, obtained new side lights and a fog light for Gloria. 'Shootin' Tom, (who welded Gloria's front mudguards) so called because he was always first to leave saying "Got to shoot off, Gladys will wonder where I am!" As if she did not know! 'Boxing' Bill, an old fist fighter, who worked at Austin, Longbridge. Harry 'Rag' dressed in a creased beige raincoat like Columbo the TV detective. Finally, my father being an electrician was called 'Sparky' Len.

I loved Gloria as much as my father did and learned a lot about cars. I fitted an aluminium waist coachline, polished the wheel trims back to metal, fitted a water temperature gauge and replacement rev-counter sourced from a scrapyard. Dad and I also painted the mudguards with black Valspar.

Gloria was used on Sundays and an annual holiday to a cottage at Bromyard. We left home at 9 a.m. had a picnic, 'half a snifter' in a few pubs and by 5 p.m. completed the 50 mile journey! During the two weeks Gloria took us to Malvern, Ledbury and Hereford, performing magnificently!

The right-hand photograph was taken during the time I learned to drive in Gloria. This was just before Harry 'Rag' bought Gloria back when my father bought a 1947 Rover 16. Since then I have been a 'Jag Man' and now the proud owner of a Jaguar 3.4-Litre Mk1 which I purchased for £50 in 1973, but that is another story!

Michael Mannering, Shropshire

Specification

Engine: 15.72 hp;
6 cylinders; 65 mm bore by
100 mm stroke; capacity
1,991 cc; overhead inlet and
side exhaust valves; twin
Solex carburettors.
Gearbox: 4 forward speeds
and reverse with free-wheel
pre-selection.
Brakes: Lockheed
hydraulically operated on all
four wheels; handbrake
operating on rear drums.
Track: 4 ft. 2 in.
Wheelbase: 9 ft. 8¹/₁₆ in.
Production: September
1934 to August 1935
Price New: £385

Featured Car

Registration Number:
AHP 616
Licensing Authority:
Coventry
Registration Date:
December 1934
Notes: From the Coventry
vehicle registration records
the club has learnt that this
Gloria was last licensed on
5th July 1954 by Tony
French from
Wolverhampton.
This car no longer exists.

GLORIA SIX VITESSE SALOON

This is a photograph of me, aged about seven, sitting on the bonnet of my father's Gloria. It was taken in around 1951 while we were on our summer holidays outside the Neptune Hotel in Hunstanton Village, Norfolk. Father was an optician in Leek, Staffordshire, and was in the habit of changing his car on a regular basis, which he bought at local auctions. Consequently, I have very few memories of this Gloria from the short time that he owned it, except that I do recall being picked up from school once by my mother – I normally used the bus.

Many of the cars that my father owned smelt of exhaust fumes and made me feel sick – the Gloria was no exception. Father was always getting the garage to check the exhaust system for leaks but none were found. It is later in life that I have come to realise that the culprit was probably piston blow-by from the open crankcase breather, and a poorly sealed engine compartment bulkhead.

It is interesting to note that, even in 1951, the offside headlight is still blanked off, probably as a result of wartime blackout regulations.

Peter Jackson, Yorkshire

GLORIA SIX VITESSE SALOON

This is my first Triumph, which I purchased some time during the late 1950s. The photograph pictures me standing proudly next to the car and was taken by my friend George in Feltham, Middlesex, where we were living at the time.

We had some great fun in those days. As far as I can recollect, I was very impressed with the performance and comfort of the car, although it did have a few mechanical problems. I cannot remember exactly the nature of these problems but they were probably associated with the fuel supply or electrics as the engine would cut out from time to time.

I eventually sold the car to a Mr Rogers who lived in Harlech Road, Southgate, just down the road from my house. He had always admired the car and I believe that he ran it for many years thereafter.

My next car was a Dolomite Roadster (*see page 110*).

Eric Whitehouse, Cornwall

Specification

Engine: 15.72 hp; 6 cylinders; 65 mm bore by 100 mm stroke; capacity 1,991 cc; overhead inlet and side exhaust valves; twin Solex carburettors.
Gearbox: 4 forward speeds and reverse with free-wheel pre-selection.
Brakes: Lockheed hydraulically operated on all four wheels; handbrake operating on rear drums.
Track: 4 ft. 2 in.
Wheelbase: 9 ft. 8$^{1}/_{16}$ in.
Production: September 1934 to August 1935
Price New: £385

Featured Car

Registration Number: AOX 994
Licensing Authority: Birmingham
Registration Date: April 1935
Notes: 44 have been recorded and seven survive with their original style bodywork.
This car no longer exists.

Specification

Engine: 15.72 hp;
6 cylinders; 65 mm bore by
100 mm stroke; capacity
1,991 cc; overhead inlet and
side exhaust valves; twin
Solex carburettors.
Gearbox: 4 forward speeds
and reverse with free-wheel
pre-selection.
Brakes: Lockheed
hydraulically operated on all
four wheels; handbrake
operating on rear drums.
Track: 4 ft. 2 in.
Wheelbase: 9 ft. 8^1/$_{16}$ in.
Production: September
1934 to August 1935
Price New: £385

Featured Car

Registration Number:
RC ????
Licensing Authority:
Derby
Registration Date:
1935
Notes: This car no longer
exists.

GLORIA SIX VITESSE SALOON

I remember when my father bought this car in 1943 when most vehicles were off the road. It was in very good order and father paid £55 which he thought was terribly dear as he never reckoned to pay more than £10 for a car! It was originally supplied by Sanderson and Holmes of Derby. Father ran the car through the war and up to the early 1950s.

This photograph was taken in 1947 and shows me (aged about sixteen) with my school friend, Bruce Jones, to my right together with my youngest brother Richard sitting on the roof. It was taken at my parents' home, White House Farm, Pleatling Magna. The dents in the front wing were caused by my mother who was about five feet four inches tall and could only just see over the dashboard!

In about 1952 my mother was going to Leicester and got stuck in some floods. She left the car in approximately six inches of water, though it was still rising, and walked to the next village where she got a taxi home. When father and I came home at midday from working on the farm we were surprised to see her there. Mother told us that the car was stuck in floods at Wigston and father said "Huh, you better take Noel (who worked for us) and the tractor to retrieve it". When we arrived we reversed the tractor up to the rear of the car and looked inside where we could see mother's hat floating level with the rear window! We had a chain with a large hook on which we managed to lower into the water and hook onto the rear bumper. This was done without either of us getting wet. Once we had pulled the car out of the flood we opened the doors and 'whoosh' all the water poured out! Although we drained all the water and fuel out and dried it as well as we could (there were no space heaters or fan heaters back then) the car never ran properly again.

Father eventually sold the car for £20 and as far as I know it was scrapped in either 1954 or 1955.

This was the first car I drove and it left such an impression that I had to buy one! Many years later I eventually found one that was surplus to requirements at a museum. It required a total restoration, which took me 14 years to complete to a very high standard (better than when it was new) and in 2005 it was back on the road.

John Marshall, Leicestershire

GLORIA SIX FLOW-FREE SALOON

Specification

Engine: 15.72 hp;
6 cylinders; 65 mm bore by
100 mm stroke; capacity
1,991 cc; overhead inlet and
side exhaust valves; twin
Solex carburettors.
Gearbox: 4 forward speeds
and reverse with free-wheel
pre-selection.
Brakes: Lockheed
hydraulically operated on all
four wheels; handbrake
operating on rear drums.
Track: 4 ft. 2 in.
Wheelbase: 9 ft. 8^1/$_{16}$ in.
Production: September
1934 to August 1935
Price New: £425

I first saw this beautiful black Gloria Flow-Free in 1948 when I was 13 years old. My family had moved from Guernsey after the war and I was staying with an aunt in Guildford while my father was house hunting. Mission accomplished, he turned up one evening to collect me in this amazing car. It was dark as we left and I will never forget the sight of the red leather seats and polished dashboard as the interior was illuminated.

Our journey along the A31 and over the Hogs Back to Ringwood in Hampshire was truly memorable. The car seemed to glide effortlessly along the road at high speed and was unbelievably quiet and comfortable.

Our new home was in Verwood, a village near Ringwood, where my father started a small market garden. I travelled with him a lot delivering produce. Wherever we went we were approached by people wanting to know about this rare car. The first photograph was taken during one of these trips alongside the A31 near Ringwood. The building shown is 'The Kettle', now long gone, and there is a Shell filling station in its place.

As I grew older I was allowed to drive the car down our private lane and, when sitting in the passenger seat with my father driving, I was allowed to steer the car and change gear. This was made easier due to the racing style gearbox which had a free-wheel pre-selector, permitting gear changes to be made without use of the clutch. Also the steering was so precise that steering round normal bends required little movement of the large steering wheel.

I have never ceased to wonder at how advanced the car was. The Coventry Climax six cylinder engine looked and sounded great, the built-in jacking system and twin batteries with a master switch fitted under the back seat were a rarity, but my favourite features were the quick release racing style chrome fuel filler caps fitted to each rear wing.

This car played a big part in my early life and the second photograph shows me (on the right) alongside the car with my stepmother and brother. Sadly the car was scrapped in 1959 to be replaced by a SS Jaguar Saloon.

Barry Vaudin, Dorset

Featured Car

Registration Number:
ARW 671
Licensing Authority:
Coventry
Registration Date:
March 1935
Notes: This car was
originally owned by the
Triumph Company Ltd.,
and featured in their
advertisement placed in the
28th June 1935 edition of
The Autocar magazine.
This car no longer exists.

Specification

Engine: 15.72 hp;
6 cylinders; 65 mm bore by
100 mm stroke; capacity
1,991 cc; overhead inlet and
side exhaust valves; twin
Solex carburettors.
Gearbox: 4 forward speeds
and reverse with free-wheel
pre-selection.
Brakes: Lockheed
hydraulically operated on all
four wheels; handbrake
operating on rear drums.
Track: 4 ft. 2 in.
Wheelbase: 9 ft. 8$^{1}/_{16}$ in.
Production: September
1934 to August 1935
Price New: £425

Featured Car

Registration Number:
BKX 748
Licensing Authority:
Buckinghamshire
Registration Date:
1935
Notes: There are no known
survivors, from the eight
recorded examples. One
body remains, rescued from
a Bentley, and that has been
beautifully restored on a
1938 2-Litre Vitesse chassis
(which is almost identical to
the original Gloria chassis).

GLORIA SIX FLOW-FREE SALOON

I bought this Gloria on 23rd April 1951 and I still have the original purchase receipt. She cost me £255 plus my Wolseley Hornet. The Gloria was painted cream with chocolate brown wings. I was not keen on this colour combination so I repainted it light grey with maroon wings. The spare wheel was mounted on the off-side front wing just behind the front wheel (I had removed it when this photograph was taken). I understand this is unusual as the majority of Flow-Frees' spare wheels were mounted in the near-side front wing.

These Glorias were very rare so imagine my surprise when I parked next to another Flow-Free later that year in Sackville Street in Manchester's city centre. I wish that I had photographed the two side by side.

Throughout the years I owned the car it was very reliable. I did however have to replace some of the ash frame where it had rotted. I took these photographs in 1951 with the Gloria parked outside my garage in Moss Side, Manchester. After I had sold the Gloria in 1955 I understand that it had two more owners before sadly it was scrapped.

I was so impressed with this Triumph I later bought two more. The first was a Gloria Six Saloon (registration number WH 6816) from an American airman based at Burtonwood (the engine and engine bay were painted American Air Force Blue!). Then in 1953 I owned a Dolomite 14/60 Saloon (registration number DVT 940). I had to replace this car's engine when I discovered that the block had cracked.

Alex Britton, Lancashire

GLORIA TOURER

Specification

Engine: 10.8 hp;
4 cylinders; 66 mm bore by
90 mm stroke; capacity
1,232 cc; overhead inlet and
side exhaust valve; single
S.U. carburettor.
Gearbox: 4 forward speeds
and reverse with free-wheel
pre-selection.
Brakes: Lockheed
hydraulically operated on all
four wheels; handbrake
operating on rear drums.
Track: 4 ft. 2 in.
Wheelbase: 9 ft.
Production: September
1934 to August 1935
Price New: £298

Featured Car

Registration Number:
VG 7543
Licensing Authority:
Norwich
Registration Date:
April 1935
Notes: Eight have been
recorded and it is estimated
that three survive with their
original style bodywork.
This car still exists and is
being restored.

Gloria was found at the end of a chicken run in the small Norfolk village of Aldborough by a local garage owner. He rebuilt her for his son for when he finished his national service in about 1956. At that time the car was painted dark blue with green interior and later his son repainted her red. Over the next few years she stayed in North Walsham, being owned by various members of the same family.

Gloria was then sold to another local family who successfully ran it for a number of years. Hazel, now my wife, actually had a ride in Gloria dressed in her bridesmaid dress at her sister's wedding in 1961. Little did she guess that it would be in our garage for 40 years. The next owner was a singer and guitar player in a local band and he managed to destroy the engine.

I purchased Gloria in 1966 for the grand sum of £8. Most of the engine was in the boot. The singer and his grandad had fitted an Austin Seven carburettor to the engine. This modification resulted in burnt out engine valves.

I worked in a local garage and thought that Gloria was 'right up my street' and I could soon repair it. I soon discovered that no parts were available, so I decided to either scrap Gloria or fit a Ford Ten engine in her. When my boss said "What's up lad?" I related the story to him and he replied: "Give me an old valve and I will see what I can do." Four weeks later he gave me a set of valves which he had made from those fitted to Hillman Tens. The engine was then rebuilt, other missing parts were made and the car was up and running again with an MoT. After a 15 mile road test all was running well, so I gave her a quick wash and polish and put her on the garage forecourt with a £25 'for sale' sign in the windscreen. Several people looked at Gloria which resulted in one person being interested but he did not want to pay the asking price.

She remained on the forecourt all winter, after which my boss wanted it moved. At this time Hazel and I decided to get married and bought a bungalow with two garages. Gloria was driven into one of the garages and I closed the doors behind her. There the car remained for the next 40 years, little loved and unappreciated, while we got on with married life and all that goes with it. I am pleased that I did not sell Gloria because now that I have retired she has given me the interesting challenge of her restoration.

Sid & Hazel Fuller, Norfolk

Specification

Engine: 10.8 hp;
4 cylinders; 66 mm bore by
90 mm stroke; capacity
1,232 cc; overhead inlet and
side exhaust valve; twin S.U.
carburettors.
Gearbox: 4 forward speeds
and reverse with free-wheel
pre-selection.
Brakes: Lockheed
hydraulically operated on all
four wheels; handbrake
operating on rear drums.
Track: 4 ft. 2 in.
Wheelbase: 9 ft.
Production: September
1934 to August 1935
Price New: £320

Featured Car

Registration Number:
BOA 90
Licensing Authority:
Birmingham
Registration Date:
May 1935
Notes: This car is one of
three possible survivors
from the six recorded.

GLORIA VITESSE TOURER

This Gloria was left in a back garden in Urmston, Manchester, with a door over it to keep the rain out and a rockery built around it to enhance the view. It had no wings, bonnet or lights and a huge hole in the chassis, otherwise it looked fine! The price for the Gloria was that we had to put the garden back together after digging it out of the rockery. Iris said that at the very least we ought to pay something for it, so we bought the owner a two shilling box of chocolates.

With the help from our friend Steve Soar and his Triumph Monte Carlo we decided to tow the Gloria home using the back roads round Old Trafford. We thought that the following Wednesday (half day closing) would be the quietest day to tow it home. We hooked up the remains of the car to the tow rope and set off. Little did we realise that Manchester United were playing at home that evening. When we approached the Old Trafford area we encountered hundreds of fans plus every cop in town! It was not long before we were pulled over by a policeman and told that if he had not been so busy he would have banned us from the road forever!

Once home we looked around the interior and found a half-crown – we were in profit! We sourced wings at a local scrapyard. These panels required 'modification' as they were from a larger six-cylinder engined Gloria. After a lot of hard work we were at last ready for the open road, with new brakes and clutch. With Iris plus our three girls hanging onto the hood, we drove up Hard Knott Pass to test the clutch and down the other side to test the brakes.

These photographs were taken at our home in Morecambe Bay. Two of our daughters, Rebecca wearing the black hat and Emma, are sitting on the bonnet. I eventually sold the Gloria in the mid to late 1970s to Tim Holt, who rebuilt it over the next five years for his wife Jenny.

Ches Chesney, Lancashire

GLORIA VITESSE TOURER

Specification

Engine: 10.8 hp;
4 cylinders; 66 mm bore by
90 mm stroke; capacity
1,232 cc; overhead inlet and
side exhaust valve; twin
S.U. carburettors.
Gearbox: 4 forward speeds
and reverse with free-wheel
pre-selection.
Brakes: Lockheed
hydraulically operated on all
four wheels; handbrake
operating on rear drums.
Track: 4 ft. 2 in.
Wheelbase: 9 ft.
Production: September
1934 to August 1935
Price New: £320

Featured Car

Registration Number:
BXP 268
Licensing Authority:
London
Registration Date:
April 1935
Notes: Gloria Vitesse
Tourers were fitted with a
different style dashboard, to
house a large rev-counter
and speedometer, compared
with the 'standard' Gloria
Tourer.
This car still exists requiring
restoration.

This cream and black Gloria was purchased by me in about 1959 from a local man named Butterworth, who had been a member of the Dolomite Association (a car club formed in the mid-1950s to help keep all models of pre-war Triumphs on the road) and came with a collection of club newsletters which made fascinating reading. The recent demise of this club inspired the beginnings of the Triumph Register in which my cousin, Glyn Lancaster Jones, and I were instrumental.

The Gloria was in very good condition and had only one serious failure. When out one day with my father we noticed the engine was rough and making grumbling noises but continued to run so we nursed it home through the traffic. Subsequent investigations showed that the crankshaft had quietly broken in two just before the flywheel. Though fractured it just managed to keep everything rotating on a light throttle to get us home. A new crankshaft was installed and no further trouble was experienced.

The left-hand photograph was taken on a caravanning holiday with Glyn and the right-hand photograph was taken in 1966.

I still own this Gloria. It is still in one piece to this day, though not on the road at present.

Roy Begent, Cheshire

Specification

Engine: 10.8 hp;
4 cylinders; 66 mm bore by
90 mm stroke; capacity
1,232 cc; overhead inlet and
side exhaust valve; twin S.U.
carburettors.
Gearbox: 4 forward speeds
and reverse with free-wheel
pre-selection.
Brakes: Lockheed
hydraulically operated on all
four wheels; handbrake
operating on rear drums.
Track: 4 ft. 2 in.
Wheelbase: 9 ft.
Production: September
1934 to August 1935
Price New: £320

Featured Car

Registration Number:
PK 43
Licensing Authority:
Malaya
Registration Date:
1934 or 1935
Notes: It is not known how
many Triumphs were
exported to Malaya. When
the question was asked of
'Bill' Billingham, Triumph's
Chief Sales Manager, he
replied that these ash
framed cars were not
successful in that part of the
world because of the
climate, plus the termites
were very fond of the wood!

GLORIA VITESSE TOURER

My father, Raja Muzaffar, was the owner of a convertible Triumph Herald in British Racing Green in the late 1960s and was, at one point, chairman of the Perak Triumph Owners Club. It also happened that his father (my grandfather), Raja Kamaralzaman Raja Mansur, had also owned a Triumph in the 1930s. At that time, Tok Kam (as my grandfather was fondly known) was in the Malayan Civil Service as the State Treasurer of the state of Perak. In those days in British Malaya, owning a car was a luxury as motor vehicles had to be imported.

The photograph on the left, which is the earliest I came across from my father's collection, is of Tok Kam's Triumph Gloria Vitesse Tourer. It was taken in 1937 at the Lake Garden in Taiping and shows my grandmother, Pah Bedah, seated behind the steering wheel. Sitting beside her was Che' An Abdullah, a close relation of the family. The other photograph, probably taken at a similar time by Tok Kam shows my father, his sister and his elder brother standing in front of the Gloria.

My father remembered clearly the red seats of the Gloria and how he felt the rear boot could fit both him and his brother (aged four and five, respectively) at that time!

Tok Kam was later installed as Raja Di-Hilir of Perak (which was second in line to the throne of the Perak Sultanate) and he parted with the Triumph Gloria as he had use of several different British and American cars, most of which were used in an official capacity.

Raja Mahariz Muzaffar, Kuala Lumpur, Malaysia

GLORIA MONTE CARLO TOURER

In early 1949, while a junior engineer in the City Engineer's Department, Bath, I accompanied an office friend to collect a 1938 Sunbeam Talbot Tourer which he had bought in Bristol. In the garage alongside the Sunbeam was this Triumph. A young man's dream! It was British Racing Green with twin spare wheels, an 18 gallon petrol tank fitted with a racing pattern lever operated filler cap (as was the radiator) and 'knock off' wheel spinners. I was hooked. A week later, with the same friend, who incidentally was teaching me to drive, we returned. I paid £135 and my adventure with the motor car had begun.

I soon realised that the hood was 'shot' and the side screens were in tatters, but who cared? In fact neither were used during the whole of my ownership. A Triumph manual, a precious gift from a friend, advised that the engine should be decarbonised every 5,000 miles! Fortunately a firm called Pride and Clarke in London could supply gaskets, valves etc. An ex-London Transport mechanic was enlisted to undertake the decoke. Finally, to make it roadworthy, the splits in the tyre walls were remedied by fitting 'gaiters' to the inner tubes, current practice then as new tyres were unobtainable.

I soon passed my driving test after some lessons in my friend's Sunbeam and some reversing and parking practise on a large forecourt. The Triumph was fitted with a 'crash' gearbox so double-declutching was the order of the day, but on those days when my timing was a bit 'off' it was a joy to engage the freewheel, allowing easy clutchless gear changes.

One episode with the car that I remember clearly was when I offered a lift home to a rather well built lady from the tennis club. Not long after seating herself heavily on the rear seat, smoke started rising beneath her. Seeing the smoke she rapidly evacuated the seat! Her weight had pressed down the steel pan supporting the seat onto one of the two batteries' terminals and had set fire to the seat. I quickly extinguished the fire and we resumed our journey.

Unfortunately the cost of the continual running repairs outstripped my modest resources and I sold the Triumph for £109 10s. I last saw the car disappear in a blue haze as the new owner 'gunned' it through the gears on his way back home in Gloucestershire.

Austin Greenhalgh, Essex

Specification

Engine: 10.8 hp; 4 cylinders; 66 mm bore by 90 mm stroke; capacity 1,232 cc; overhead inlet and side exhaust valve; twin 'easy start' down-draught carburettors.
Gearbox: 4 forward speeds and reverse with free-wheel pre-selection.
Brakes: Lockheed hydraulically operated on all four wheels; handbrake operating on rear drums.
Track: 4 ft.
Wheelbase: 9 ft.
Production: July 1934 to August 1935
Price New: £335

Featured Car

Registration Number: BHU 802
Licensing Authority: Bristol
Registration Date: Between April and June 1935
Notes: Nine have been recorded and it is thought that three survive with their original style bodywork. This car no longer exists.

Specification

Engine: 10.8 hp;
4 cylinders; 66 mm bore by
90 mm stroke; capacity
1,232 cc; overhead inlet and
side exhaust valve; twin
'easy start' down-draught
carburettors.
Gearbox: 4 forward speeds
and reverse with free-wheel
pre-selection.
Brakes: Lockheed
hydraulically operated on all
four wheels; handbrake
operating on rear drums.
Track: 4 ft.
Wheelbase: 9 ft.
Production: July 1934 to
August 1935
Price New: £335

Featured Car

Registration Number:
BGK 10
Licensing Authority:
London
Registration Date:
July 1934
Notes: This was one of two
1935 models that was a
'carry-over' from the
previous year's range. The
only change to the Monte
Carlo was the fitment of the
new style radiator surround.
The other model to be
similarly treated was the
Gloria Ten Saloon.
This car no longer exists.

I owned this Gloria from about 1957 to 1960. I cannot remember where I bought it from or for how much, but I do remember that it was brush painted green. During these years I was training as a nurse at the Lister Hospital in Hitchin and was making frequent journeys in the Gloria between there and home, the village store at Old Weston in Huntingdonshire. On one such journey I had to stop quickly when the cabin filled with acrid smoke – I had forgotten to remove the sack that I kept over the engine during winter nights!

My Gloria came with one complete spare wheel and one spare tyre, both held on by a leather strap. Sadly I lost the tyre when the strap came loose on a 'show off trip' around the villages. I never did find that tyre!

Most of my courting was by virtue of this car. The object of my attention was also a nurse named Sheila who eventually became my wife for 46 years. Those old Triumphs were effective in more ways than one! My father-in-law Daniel Booth was manager of Burtons in Hitchin – a bowler hat and rolled umbrella man. He became a great friend. However, senior readership will appreciate that in the 1950s 10 pm was frequently the time to end courting and quietness was important. Many times I coasted the last hundred yards to Sheila's home and then pushed the Gloria another 50 yards before starting the engine!

Courting took us to Keswick and the narrow lanes of the Lake District. The left-hand photo of me and the Gloria was taken at the top of Dunmall Raise between Grasmere and Thirlmere. One morning during this trip the car would not start. I eventually found the problem to be a blocked exhaust pipe. It was either a teenage prank or more likely that I had reversed into a bank and filled the pipe with Cumbrian soil.

The two ladies photographed in the front of my Gloria were visiting aunts from Lancashire. Neither were drivers but they enjoyed being photographed as if they were!

Eventually I sold the Gloria for £30 to a friend at the hospital. The money helped with funding our wedding. Shortly afterwards the MoT was introduced and the Gloria failed on kingpins. My friend could not afford the repair, so the Gloria was scrapped!

Kevan Ashton, Lincolnshire

GLORIA SOUTHERN CROSS 2-SEATER

Specification

Engine: 10.8 hp;
4 cylinders; 66 mm bore by
90 mm stroke; capacity
1,232 cc; overhead inlet and
side exhaust valve; twin
S.U. carburettors.
Gearbox: 4 forward speeds
and reverse with free-wheel
pre-selection.
Brakes: Lockheed
hydraulically operated on all
four wheels; handbrake
operating on rear drums.
Track: 4 ft. 2 in.
Wheelbase: 8 ft.
Production: August 1934 to
July 1935
Price New: £275

Featured Car

Registration Number:
BNB 25
Licensing Authority:
Manchester
Registration Date:
February 1935
Notes: This car exists in
fine restored condition and
is enjoying regular use in
Portugal.

BNB 25 was bought from a used car dealer in Peterborough in 1963 for £60. Even then this car was well past the first flush of youth and at the age of 28, some nine years older than me. It was my parents idea that I should have a car – I was perfectly happy with my 250 cc James motorcycle, but it was becoming increasingly evident that my riding style and general approach to life wouldn't see me past my 20th birthday.

We towed the car back to our home in Brampton. Dad, who was a first-class mechanic (he looked after his employer's two Bugattis, a type 37A and a 51B) was unhappy with the sound of the engine and wanted to look at it. So we took it all apart, fitted new piston rings and I learned a lot about grinding in valves.

At this point it occurred to me that I should do something about learning to drive. Only dad and my pal Brian Betts were prepared to fulfil this role, which was not without its hazards. On a night out with Brian we were coming back from a pub well past closing time and it was very dark. The car had no instrument lights, so I couldn't see the oil pressure gauge. "What's that smell?" said Brian. "I dunno" I said, my thought processes dulled by the several hours spent in the pub. By the time we got home all was clearly not well with the engine. Dad's opinion was sought. "You've run the bearings" he said, not impressed with either of us. Dad repaired it in time for my driving test. This time though, I learned all about white metal bearings and big ends.

The day of my test arrived and with the examiner riding shotgun we set off around the streets of Wellingborough and it started to rain. With no hood on the car a wet looking examiner said "You've passed", clearly not wishing to go through it again at a later date!

One night Tina, my girlfriend at the time, and I had not parted on good terms. Driving home to Brampton and going far too fast around a bend I lost control. The car spun a couple of times and we careered stern first through a brick garden wall, ending up in a flowerbed. Having had too much to drink, in the eyes of the law, it seemed appropriate to drive back out through the hole in the wall and worry about it later. The next morning I walked back and met the homeowner and a policeman, who were clearing bricks off the road and looking at the remains of some roses. "I'm afraid I'm responsible" I said. They were pretty decent about it and seemed to accept my explanation about swerving to avoid a dog. After agreeing to pay for the damage, I returned home to check BNB 25. The rear number plate was hanging off, a wheel was buckled and worst of all, I'd destroyed the rear tray that the two spare wheels sat in. Thankfully it was all repaired. Sometime later I received a letter from the Chief Constable, clearly not an animal lover himself, telling me not to do it again.

Later I met my future wife, Glenys, the younger daughter of an RAF family. BNB 25 was our wedding car as we drove away from Brampton Church to take up married life in Berkshire.

Dick McClary, Hampshire

Specification

Engine: 10.8 hp;
4 cylinders; 66 mm bore by
90 mm stroke; capacity
1,232 cc; overhead inlet and
side exhaust valve; twin
S.U. carburettors.
Gearbox: 4 forward speeds
and reverse with free-wheel
pre-selection.
Brakes: Lockheed
hydraulically operated on all
four wheels; handbrake
operating on rear drums.
Track: 4 ft. 2 in.
Wheelbase: 8 ft.
Production: August 1934 to
July 1935
Price New: £275

Featured Car

Registration Number:
ARW 731
Licensing Authority:
Coventry
Registration Date:
March 1935
Notes: From the Coventry
vehicle registration records
the club has learnt that this
Gloria was last licensed on
3rd January 1959 by John
W. Richards from North
Wingfield, Derbyshire.
This car no longer exists.

GLORIA SOUTHERN CROSS 2-SEATER

ARW 731 is shown being driven by J. P. Ferguson and navigated by my father Sidney Elgar in the 1935 Exeter Trial (left) and successfully climbing Simms in the MCC Torquay Trial on 18th July 1936 (right).

J .P. Ferguson (Ferg), who's beautifully detailed cut-away drawings can still be found in back copies of *The Autocar* and other motoring publications, was later to become my sister's godfather. Unfortunately I know little of the history of his association with this car but I found the photographs amongst my father's papers.

Suffice to say that Ferg and my father were great friends before the war and obviously enjoyed their motoring competition activities. It says much for the quality of the Southern Cross, as well as the capability of the driver, that they managed to 'clean' Simms. Those who are familiar with trials driving, or riding, in the West Country will know what a fearsome reputation this 1 in 3.5 hill has.

This car was followed by Ferg's Southern Cross, registered CKV 560, which then became my father's car and eventually mine (*see pages 85 and 86*).

Ed Elgar, Hampshire

GLORIA SOUTHERN CROSS 2-SEATER

Specification

Engine: 10.8 hp;
4 cylinders; 66 mm bore by
90 mm stroke; capacity
1,232 cc; overhead inlet and
side exhaust valve; twin S.U.
carburettors.
Gearbox: 4 forward speeds
and reverse with free-wheel
pre-selection.
Brakes: Lockheed
hydraulically operated on all
four wheels; handbrake
operating on rear drums.
Track: 4 ft. 2 in.
Wheelbase: 8 ft.
Production: August 1934 to
July 1935
Price New: £275

Featured Car

Registration Number:
WF 7712
Licensing Authority:
Yorkshire, East Riding
Registration Date:
May 1935
Notes: 30 have been
recorded and 14 survive
with their original style
bodywork.
This car still exists and
currently requires
restoration to return it to
roadworthy condition.

I purchased this two-tone blue Gloria in 1959 for £50. As a result of my 'spirited' driving style I had several incidents in the car in which I was lucky to escape unscathed and with the Gloria intact. The first of these was when I was driving home to Stratford-upon-Avon on a summer's evening. Without warning the rear near-side wheel parted company and rolled at high speed into Nightingale Wood. At the same time I was grinding to a halt in a shower of sparks from the brake drum which was now acting as the fourth wheel! A neighbour of mine, travelling in his Austin A35, spotted me at the side of the road and stopped to help. Between us we jacked up the Gloria, wound some insulation tape round the damaged splined hub and forced one of the two spare wheels on with a hammer! This lash-up got me home and soon after I managed to source a second hand hub in better condition.

The Gloria's brakes were very effective and with this in mind I often drove with the free-wheel engaged. This was fine until one day when driving back to Stratford-upon-Avon at about 60 mph. I approached a T-junction and braked hard. There was a bang and grinding noise from one of the wheels (a hub had stripped its splines). With this sudden reduction in braking I careered straight across the junction, smashed through a five bar gate and eventually came to a halt about 60 feet into a green field. I was very lucky that there was no other traffic back at the junction, otherwise I might not be telling this story!

The final lucky escape I can recall was when a throttle linkage broke, causing one of the carburettors to stick open. It happened just as I was approaching a roundabout. There was no chance of negotiating it in the normal way, so straight over the top I went. As the Gloria hit the roundabout we were launched into the air at about 30 degrees, landed in the middle and drove off the other side. Luckily no damage was suffered to the car or me but the roundabout's bedding plants did not look as good afterwards!

Eventually in 1965 I sold the Gloria and a van load of spares to a chap in Lincolnshire for the same price I paid for her.

Bernard Bollons, Warwickshire

Specification

Engine: 10.8 hp;
4 cylinders; 66 mm bore by
90 mm stroke; capacity
1,232 cc; overhead inlet and
side exhaust valve; twin
S.U. carburettors.
Gearbox: 4 forward speeds
and reverse with free-wheel
pre-selection.
Brakes: Lockheed
hydraulically operated on all
four wheels; handbrake
operating on rear drums.
Track: 4 ft. 2 in.
Wheelbase: 8 ft.
Production: August 1934 to
July 1935
Price New: £275

Featured Car

Registration Number:
WS 5995
Licensing Authority:
Edinburgh
Registration Date:
September 1935
Notes: This car was owned
and successfully campaigned
in Scottish rallies and trials
by Mr W. J. Lamb during
the late 1940s. As the only
Triumph competing he won
the MG Car Club's 1947
Moorfoot Sporting Rally.
This car still exists and is
currently being restored.

GLORIA SOUTHERN CROSS 2-SEATER

In the early 1960s a friend at work told me of a car with the name of a film star that was for sale. I was told that the price was £30 if it started and £15 if it did not (my wages at that time were £9 a week). When I saw the car it was love at first sight. It had stood by a wall of a house for many years in Rochdale. The half of the car away from the wall that could be reached was painted racing green with black mudguards and the other half had been left to rust. This two seater was impractical as we had just had our first child Sarah, but hey, we could put her on the ledge at the back. I really wanted the car but still had to sell my idea to my wife Iris!

The owner couldn't start the Gloria so £15 it was. A neighbour towed it to our home which was on a new housing estate. I installed two new batteries, pressed the start button and it roared into life. I initially painted the rest of the Gloria racing green to nearly match the other half and then later painted it entirely red. It became our family transport and was driven every day to work. The neighbours on the estate used to laugh at its condition but often asked for help to tow start their car, sheepishly I might add!

In the evenings when Sarah wouldn't go to sleep we put her on the tool box behind the seats and drove the car around the block. To the sound of the tappets (or was it the exhaust fumes?) she would fall fast asleep. Gloria always passed her MoT without a problem and we had lots of fun with her. We would get wet when it rained and brown when the sun shone. In these photographs I can be seen with Sarah in the passenger seat and Iris behind the steering wheel.

When the Pre-1940 Triumph Owners Club was formed we met up with Glyn Lancaster Jones and with his help fitted a replacement engine and gearbox. Steve Soar (who had a Monte Carlo) rewired it, but all the wires were covered with red sleeving!

In 1968 we moved to Morecambe Bay with the Gloria towing our second Triumph, a 4-Seater Tourer (*see page 59*).

I sold the Gloria in the mid 1970s to fellow Triumph enthusiast Brian Bishop in Warwickshire.

Ches Chesney, Lancashire

GLORIA SIX SOUTHERN CROSS 2-SEATER

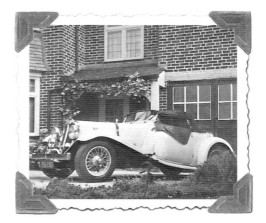

Specification

Engine: 15.72 hp;
6 cylinders; 65 mm bore by
100 mm stroke; capacity
1,991 cc; overhead inlet and
side exhaust valves; twin
S.U. carburettors.
Gearbox: 4 forward speeds
and reverse with free-wheel
pre-selection.
Brakes: Lockheed
hydraulically operated on all
four wheels; handbrake
operating on rear drums.
Track: 4 ft. 2 in.
Wheelbase: 8 ft. 8$^{1}/_{16}$ in.
Production: September
1934 to August 1936
Price New: £335

In 1945 I found this Triumph in an old barn in Warwickshire. It had belonged to a young man who sadly had been killed during the Second World War. If my memory serves me correctly, his mother gave me £5 to take the car away as it continued to bring back the sad memories of her loss.

The car had deteriorated to a dreadful state as it had been used as a fowl pen and became home to various rodents. It was so bad that I restored it from the chassis up. I also gave the engine a mild tune up which included flowing the head, raising the compression ratio, fitting a free flowing exhaust system and many other mild tweaks.

After taking a year to restore and to carry out the various modifications, I covered over 80,000 miles in the following six years without a single mishap. I remember it being a very quick car compared with other cars on the road in the late 1940s and early 1950s. My future wife and I derived great pleasure from the Triumph, together with our many friends, charging around the countryside and coastal resorts most weekends (as can be seen from the left-hand photograph, taken on one such occasion).

In 1952 I got married and used the Triumph for the last time on our honeymoon. I decided to sell the Triumph and obtain something more suitable for my growing business interests. One of my business ventures included founding and running 'Broadspeed', a company initially preparing and entering Minis for circuit racing (as well as being the 'Governor' I was also one of the drivers in our team). By the mid 1960s we had switched to using Fords. In the 1970s Broadspeed entered the British Touring Car Championship with entries including Ford Escorts and Capris, Jaguar XJ12 Coupés and Triumph Dolomite Sprints. During this period I had a young engineer working for me by the name of Andy Rouse. I helped and encouraged him with his racing ambitions and Andy later became a four times British Touring Car Championship winner, most notably in the 1980s driving Ford Sierra Cosworths.

Ralph Broad, Portugal

Featured Car

Registration Number:
YG 9910
Licensing Authority:
Yorkshire, West Riding
Registration Date:
January 1935
Notes: Ten have been
recorded, with most having
a competition history, and
five still exist with their
original style bodywork.
This car's bumper would
not have been fitted as
standard.
This car no longer survives.

Specification

Engine: 15.72 hp; 6 cylinders; 65 mm bore by 100 mm stroke; capacity 1,991 cc; overhead inlet and side exhaust valves; twin S.U. carburettors.
Gearbox: 4 forward speeds and reverse with free-wheel pre-selection.
Brakes: Lockheed hydraulically operated on all four wheels; handbrake operating on rear drums.
Track: 4 ft. 2 in.
Wheelbase: 8 ft. 8¹/₁₆ in.
Production: September 1934 to August 1936
Price New: £335

Featured Car

Registration Number: AAC 256
Licensing Authority: Warwickshire
Registration Date: July 1935
Notes: Apart from the Super-Charged Dolomite Straight Eight this was Triumph's most potent sports car during the 1930s. This car still survives in fine condition and is now in Singapore.

GLORIA SIX SOUTHERN CROSS 2-SEATER

These photographs of my green and black Gloria were taken circa 1961/62 at my parents' house in Truro, Cornwall. The first shows me behind the steering wheel and my mother in the passenger seat. At this distance in time my memories of ownership are a bit hazy but, as the first car that I owned and one which needed considerable rebuilding both in terms of the bodywork (which was rather battered when I first saw it) and in regard to the engine (it had been lying idle for some time) I have fond memories of the vehicle. The Gloria's previous owner lived in the village of Chacewater near Truro. Its earlier history is very sketchy, although someone that I spoke to seemed to think that it might originally have been owned by one of the Healey brothers from Perranporth.

The 1¹/₂-litre engine (which may have been a replacement as this model was produced with a 2-litre engine) needed a complete 'decoke' and tune before it would start and some serious injection of 'Plusgas' into the twin 1¹/₂ inch SUs. In fact, the car had several duplicated items: twin fuse boxes, twin HT coils and twin (electric) fuel pumps. The brakes were reasonably effective but the car itself was quite heavy and took quite a lot of stopping. Not that it was particularly fast, but I do remember the engine as being very smooth and it would start away in fourth on the flat without any judder. The fuel was held in a large slab tank at the back. As an impoverished student I never discovered the actual capacity as, even in those far-off days of petrol at 5/- a gallon, I could only ever afford to put in a few gallons to slosh around at the bottom! The gearbox was operated by quite a pleasant remote short-throw lever fairly close to hand.

I cannot remember how much I paid for the car but I have just found my original insurance document which shows an estimated value of £100 and a renewal premium of £10 2s. 6d for third party, fire and theft cover!

In use it proved pretty reliable although the handling was on the heavy side. The exhaust had very little in the way of silencing. As a result the engine produced a very satisfying deep rumble, especially when it was 'opened up'. I only recollect one anxious moment when the engine cut out and I opened up the bonnet to discover petrol flooding out of one of the carburettors (the result of a stuck float). No great disaster in itself but I seem to remember that the exhaust manifold was lower down on the same side which could have been very nasty!

Tony Smith, Devon

GLORIA TWELVE SALOON

My father owned a 1937 1½-litre Gloria Saloon from new for 25 years and in that time he covered over 200,000 miles. In about 1960 I heard from my friend, who owned a Gloria Tourer, of another Gloria for sale near Frinton and being influenced by father's favourable experience with his, of course I was keen to buy it. The car was in very good condition for 24 years old so without hesitation I bought it for £70 and sold my Austin Ten.

I lived in Hutton, Essex, and used the car for travelling to and from work in Brentwood where I worked as a motor engineer for Brentwood Engineering who were BMC car dealers. In total I travelled about 35,000 miles in the Gloria and enjoyed every minute. The road holding and brakes were superb and performance was good for a modest sized engine.

After several years of constant use the bodywork started to look tired and required a few repairs. I restored the bodywork to a high standard and gave it a fresh coat of black paint. I was so pleased with the end result that I was now reluctant to leave the car in car parks in case it was damaged. With this in mind I felt the Gloria had become a potential liability as everyday transport and not being able to afford to run a second car I reluctantly decided it had to be sold. I drove it to an auction held in Kent during 1970 where it was sold for £350.

I have always regretted selling the Gloria. Even though I no longer own a pre-war Triumph I continue to be a member of the Pre-1940 Triumph Owners Club and now intend to buy another Gloria or Vitesse should the right car become available.

Guy Hutchinson, East Sussex

Specification

Engine: 10.8 hp; 4 cylinders; 66 mm bore by 90 mm stroke; capacity 1,232 cc; overhead inlet and side exhaust valve; single S.U. carburettor.
Gearbox: 4 forward speeds and reverse with free-wheel pre-selection.
Brakes: Lockheed hydraulically operated on all four wheels; handbrake operating on rear drums.
Track: 4 ft. 2 in.
Wheelbase: 9 ft.
Production: September 1935 to August 1937
Price New: £315

Featured Car

Registration Number: J 1611
Licensing Authority: Jersey
Registration Date: 1936
Notes: This Gloria was re-registered in Devon as FTA 23 when it was brought over to mainland Britain in September 1939. This car is now in Holland awaiting restoration.

Specification

Engine: 10.8 hp;
4 cylinders; 66 mm bore by
90 mm stroke; capacity
1,232 cc; overhead inlet and
side exhaust valve; single
S.U. carburettor.
Gearbox: 4 forward speeds
and reverse with free-wheel
pre-selection.
Brakes: Lockheed
hydraulically operated on all
four wheels; handbrake
operating on rear drums.
Track: 4 ft. 2 in.
Wheelbase: 9 ft.
Production: September
1935 to August 1937
Price New: £315

Featured Car

Registration Number:
CTO 700
Licensing Authority:
Nottingham
Registration Date:
1936
Notes: This car still exists,
but the engine has been
replaced with a Wolseley
2½-litre six-cylinder unit
and the bodywork has been
removed. A four-seater
wooden tourer body is now
fitted.

GLORIA TWELVE SALOON

This blue Gloria was bought in 1964 to replace my father's previous Gloria *(described on page 43)* which needed much work. It was advertised in the Halifax area as suitable for spares. When asked what would happen to the car after any parts had been sold, the owner reckoned it would be pushed into the ravine at the back of the houses and forgotten. An offer was made marginally above the agreed price for the parts we wanted and the whole car was ours. Behind can be seen my Gloria Vitesse Tourer *(described on page 60)*, which now had the job of towing this car home. The lad who owned it is seen here in the sheepskin jacket next to me. My father, Mervyn, is just visible kneeling down in front of us looking at something. The photograph was taken by Glyn Lancaster Jones who accompanied us.

The Gloria was towed gingerly through Mytholmroyd with my father steering. What we soon found out was that he turned the key and gently let the clutch up, and it was now following under its own steam for the 25 miles home. This took quite a load off my Tourer. It was felt advisable to keep the tow-rope attached in case the fuel ran out and it was neither licensed nor insured.

The car ran reliably and well until part of the chassis frame fractured just before my father died in 1969. It was eventually moved to Glyn's mill at Todmorden and was later sold to a new owner.

Roy Begent, Cheshire

71

GLORIA TWELVE SALOON

Specification

Engine: 10.8 hp;
4 cylinders; 66 mm bore by
90 mm stroke; capacity
1,232 cc; overhead inlet and
side exhaust valve; single
S.U. carburettor.
Gearbox: 4 forward speeds
and reverse with free-wheel
pre-selection.
Brakes: Lockheed
hydraulically operated on all
four wheels; handbrake
operating on rear drums.
Track: 4 ft. 2 in.
Wheelbase: 9 ft.
Production: September
1935 to August 1937
Price New: £315

Featured Car

Registration Number:
BFM 608
Licensing Authority:
Chester
Registration Date:
1937
Notes: Kenneth Kohler
helped run the Dolomite
Association (a club formed
in 1955 to help pre-war
Triumph owners keep their
cars on the road) as editor
for their newsletter. The
club was wound-up in 1960
when the majority of
Triumphs came to the end
of their life.
This car no longer exists.

When living in my home town of Edinburgh I bought this Gloria in 1953 for £75. It was in need of a polish and a couple of tyres but fortunately there was no sign of disintegrating wood in the body.

After a couple of relatively relaxed and trouble free motoring years my wife and I decided that we would holiday in Venice. We left our baby with her doting grandparents, put patches on the patches of the Dunlop seat cushions, fitted a roof rack and set off with a veritable harem – my wife, her sister and her sister's friend (both student nurses). At 400 miles and 7 am we were in the Old Kent Road on part of my ill-chosen route through London en-route to Dover. It was sheeting rain, the road was greasy and a big dog decided to cross the road. I managed to stop but an on-coming motorcycle combination got into an uncontrollable pirouette. The nose of the sidecar wrecked my driver's door and went on to lift the front mudguard. While the nurses were marvelling that the motorcyclist miraculously needed no first aid, my wife got out and shook her fist at him crying "you've spoilt our holiday!". I was still shaking broken glass out of my shirt when the dog decided it preferred our side of the road after all. A lorry approaching from behind locked up its brakes and shunted our car onto the pavement and almost through a pub window.

Even in those days, London Police didn't come out to a road accident unless someone was hurt. They suggested on the phone that I contacted my insurance company. I discovered that the car still motored safely and proceeded to their head office on Bank Corner. A limo drove up and parked behind causing even further traffic confusion. A bowler-hatted, pinstriped manager got out and ordered me to move my pile of junk before he phoned the police. Then the sight of my wife's anguish affected him. He ordered me inside the portals and immediately he enquired whether the car would make it to Croydon. "Of course, we are going to Venice!" He picked up a phone from a desk and after a inaudible discussion he came over and told me his son had a garage in Croydon and was a wonder with crashed cars. The repairs would all be on the comprehensive insurance.

We arrived at this garage during the morning tea break, by lunchtime the boss had located a door and the front wing was straightened. A painter sprayed the door black while a 'tame gorilla' straightened the bumper. By 6 pm we were en-route for Dover. After this eventful start we made it to Venice and back without major mishaps. The above photographs were taken during the holiday outside the Palace in Fontainebleau near Paris and a street in St Jean-de-Maurienne, a village at the foot of the Mont Cenis Pass.

I eventually replaced the Gloria with a more powerful Dolomite later in the 1950s.

Ken Kohler, Dundee

Specification

Engine: 10.8 hp;
4 cylinders; 66 mm bore by
90 mm stroke; capacity
1,232 cc; overhead inlet and
side exhaust valve; twin S.U.
carburettors.
Gearbox: 4 forward speeds
and reverse with free-wheel
pre-selection.
Brakes: Lockheed
hydraulically operated on all
four wheels; handbrake
operating on rear drums.
Track: 4 ft. 2 in.
Wheelbase: 9 ft.
Production: September
1935 to August 1936
Price New: £315

Featured Car

Registration Number:
YS 8740
Licensing Authority:
Glasgow
Registration Date:
1936
Notes: 43 have been
recorded and four survive
with their original style
bodywork. It is likely that
only two of these will be
restored. These six-light
Glorias' low survival rate is
partially due to their
comparatively staid
appearance against the other
'sportier' looking Glorias.
This car no longer exists.

GLORIA TWELVE SIX-LIGHT SALOON

This Gloria, purchased by my father in 1953, was our first family car and he, now aged 87, still remembers it well. My family are from Uddingston and father was an engineer in a large factory in Glasgow. When he felt that he could afford a car he consulted the company's resident motor mechanic (who looked after the company cars) for advice. He duly obliged and recommended this Triumph.

This photograph was taken by my mother soon after its purchase. My memories of the Gloria start with the smell of its leather seats and wooden veneered dashboard and although I was only seven years old at the time I can also remember what a thrill it was to travel in. At weekends it was a family affair: up early on a Saturday morning, mother and grandmother preparing food, father and grandfather preparing the car and my brother and I standing around waiting for the 'off'. Normally we drove out to the country and coast in Ayrshire.

Our annual holiday was a big event, again with all the family, and each year we would drive to Stonehaven in north east Scotland. I remember the car boot depth was shallow and the boot lid opened down so that it could be used as a shelf. This was ideal for the wicker basket we used for the majority of our holiday clothes. When full this basket was secured on the back of the car and driven to our local railway station to be taken by train to our holiday destination. Since there were six of us travelling in Gloria, with our luggage sent on ahead it allowed for a more comfortable ride to Stonehaven. To me the journey seemed to take forever, but six hours would be realistic. On the way we would stop for lunch by the river in Perth. With our methylated spirit stove lit, placed inside a large biscuit tin (acting as an effective windbreak), we soon had the tea kettle boiling!

We kept Gloria for about eight years until father was entitled to a company car. Father sold the car to one of his friends who eventually scrapped it when he emigrated to Canada.

It has been a pleasurable experience reminiscing, as I never thought that after some 50 years I would be recounting some of the happiest days of my childhood in which Gloria played such an important part.

Scott Loudon, Derbyshire

GLORIA TWELVE VITESSE SALOON

My memories of this Gloria that my father used as everyday transport from 1955 to 1962 are a bit sketchy as are these photographs of my parents and I alongside the car sometime in the mid-1950s when I was about five or six years old.

As my father was a time-served mechanic he did his own repairs. I remember being with him on a test run after he had done some work on the rear brakes, when a wheel overtook us! The rear of the car came down with a crash and we travelled along for a short distance on the rear near-side brake drum. A classic case of stripped splines on the hub. After the wheel was retrieved and replaced we gently returned home where I assume he replaced the hub with one from the Gloria Six Cylinder Coupé (which I now understand was an extremely rare model with only one survivor) that he had broken up for spares.

One modification that I recall was to improve the lighting for his daily 12-mile journey to work in Aberdeen. This he did by making a couple of rings from sheet aluminium so that he could fit double dipping seven inch pre-focused headlight units inside the standard headlight rims.

The car had a distinctive exhaust note and I well remember our Labrador getting up from the middle of the drive and waiting at the roadside long before any of us mere humans could detect any noise. She had already heard the Gloria coming out of the village about a mile away when my father was on his way home from work.

Sadly, after father sold the Gloria, it was stolen and totally written off after colliding with a telegraph pole and was then broken for scrap. Father did go to see the Gloria with the idea of repairing it but the damage was so severe that it would not have been possible.

Richard Singer, Aberdeenshire

Specification

Engine: 10.8 hp; 4 cylinders; 66 mm bore by 90 mm stroke; capacity 1,232 cc; overhead inlet and side exhaust valve; twin S.U. carburettors.
Gearbox: 4 forward speeds and reverse with free-wheel pre-selection.
Brakes: Lockheed hydraulically operated on all four wheels; handbrake operating on rear drums.
Track: 4 ft. 2 in.
Wheelbase: 9 ft.
Production: September 1935 to August 1936
Price New: £345

Featured Car

Registration Number: CLE 998
Licensing Authority: London
Registration Date: November 1935
Notes: 41 have been recorded and four survive with their original style bodywork. It is puzzling that so few still exist when there are 18 survivors of the previous year's equivalent model.
This car no longer exists.

Specification

Engine: 10.8 hp;
4 cylinders; 66 mm bore by
90 mm stroke; capacity
1,232 cc; overhead inlet and
side exhaust valve; twin S.U.
carburettors.
Gearbox: 4 forward speeds
and reverse with free-wheel
pre-selection.
Brakes: Lockheed
hydraulically operated on all
four wheels; handbrake
operating on rear drums.
Track: 4 ft. 2 in.
Wheelbase: 8 ft.
Production: September
1935 to August 1936
Price New: £325

Featured Car

Registration Number:
CND 49
Licensing Authority:
Manchester
Registration Date:
May 1936
Notes:19 have been
recorded and it is estimated
that three survive with their
original style bodywork.
Donald Healey entered a
similar Gloria, fitted with a
1½-litre engine, in the 1937
Monte Carlo Rally. He
retired from the rally
following an accident.
This featured car still exists.

GLORIA TWELVE VITESSE SHORT SALOON

These photos were taken between 1938 and 1940 by Neville Joyce (the second owner of this Gloria) in Crewe, Cheshire, and in Rhyl, North Wales, and feature his family.

Neville was an engineer at the Rolls-Royce factory initially in Derby and later at Crewe. He was instrumental in the fact that Rolls-Royce Motor Cars changed over to using Avon tyres (due to him being impressed with his Gloria's handling characteristics when using different tyres) when he was working in the experimental department.

In the mid 1950s the ownership of this Gloria passed to Frederick Parker, another Rolls-Royce employee. Unfortunately in 1967 the car ended up in a scrapyard due to the dreaded MoT test. Here it remained unloved but not alone! Its stable mate was a post-war Triumph Renown.

This is where I came in during 1972 after a tip-off about two cars ripe for restoration from a very well meaning college lecturer. When asked by me what was the difference between the Renown, a family four-door saloon, and the Gloria, a two-door coupé and supposedly an ex-Manchester City police car, guess what this boy racer decided to go for? Yes you guessed, the Gloria. After all there was no 'street-cred' in a family saloon and the Gloria was older as well.

Needless to say 30 plus years along the line I now know why the Gloria was in the scrapyard! But I still don't regret it. The restoration continues and one day it will be completed!

Pete Woodcock, Stoke-on-Trent

GLORIA 2-LITRE VITESSE SIX-LIGHT SALOON

My uncle, Joe Brodie, bought this light cream and black Gloria in the 1930s and used it to drive to the local cattle markets either side of the Second World War. He was also permitted to drive it during the war when he was a member of the War Agricultural Committee in Northamptonshire. In 1951 he bought an Austin Sheerline and sold the Gloria to me. I took these photographs soon after at Southfield Farm, Barton Seagrave, which was my home before I married.

The Gloria had no heater, but making a large hole in the bulkhead as people did with ex-army Hillman 'Tillies' would have been sacrilege with such a fine car, so I carried ex-horse trap rugs to cover adventurous ladies on cold winter nights. It also had no windscreen de-mister, so during cold weather I kept a large potato, cut in half, and a bottle of glycerine in the Gloria and these I would rub onto the windscreen to keep it from icing up.

The Coventry Climax engine gave no trouble, but the knock on wire wheels tended to shear their splines if I did not regularly check the spinners for tightness. Another item that required regular attention was the sliding roof drainage channels which I blew out regularly, otherwise the rain water would build up and drip on the rear passengers. A very useful feature were the mechanical scissor jacks fitted on each axle. With their aid I could change a wheel very quickly.

The free-wheel was a joy to use. It was selected by a short lever just behind the gear lever and with it engaged, gear changes could be made without the use of the clutch. I found the smoothest technique was to take my foot off the accelerator select a gear, up or down, and then accelerate away. On approaching hills where engine braking was required, I found it best to disengage the freewheel whilst the engine was pulling, not freewheeling.

I remember one year travelling down to see the London to Brighton veteran car run early in the morning. Whilst driving through Luton I rounded a tight corner which made the tyres squeal. This noise caught the attention of a policeman on foot patrol who put his hand up. I pulled over and he gave me a lecture on driving too fast through town!

In 1954 I sold the Gloria to my friend, Gillian Shatford, who lived in Peterborough.

John Clarke, Northamptonshire

Specification

Engine: 15.72 hp; 6 cylinders; 65 mm bore by 100 mm stroke; capacity 1,991 cc; overhead inlet and side exhaust valves; twin S.U. carburettors.
Gearbox: 4 forward speeds and reverse with free-wheel pre-selection.
Brakes: Lockheed hydraulically operated on all four wheels; handbrake operating on rear drums.
Track: 4 ft. 2 in.
Wheelbase: 9 ft. 8$\frac{1}{16}$ in.
Production: September 1935 to August 1936
Price New: £425

Featured Car

Registration Number: CYK 136
Licensing Authority: London
Registration Date: July 1936
Notes: Three have been recorded and none survive. This model and the the Foursome Drophead Coupé were the only two 1935/6 models that Triumph did not body themselves. These were coachbuilt by Cross & Ellis.

Engine: 10.8 hp;
4 cylinders; 66 mm bore by
90 mm stroke; capacity
1,232 cc; overhead inlet and
side exhaust valve; twin
S.U. carburettors.

Gearbox: 4 forward speeds
and reverse with free-wheel
pre-selection.

Brakes: Lockheed
hydraulically operated on all
four wheels; handbrake
operating on rear drums.

Track: 4 ft. 2 in.

Wheelbase: 9 ft.

Production: September
1935 to August 1937

Price New: £325

Featured Car

Registration Number:
SU 3305

Licensing Authority:
Kincardine

Registration Date:
January 1937

Notes: 15 have been
recorded and seven survive
with their original style
bodywork. For the 1935/6
model range these Tourers'
rear bumpers were optional.
This car still exists in
unrestored condition and
was the first car registered in
Kincardine, Scotland,
during 1937.

GLORIA TWELVE VITESSE TOURER

Sometime in 1963 an MoT testing station owner, who knew that my father had owned a Gloria Saloon for some years, phoned to ask if he could buy my father's spare 10.8 h.p. engine. He had been tipped off that my father still had the spare engine in need of repair and he cheekily offered £5 for it in running order. Although quite hard up and in need of the money, when my father found out that the engine was required for a Gloria Tourer he said the engine was not for sale but would be prepared to pay him £5 for the car. His offer was accepted and within a couple of weeks father became the owner of a rather sad Tourer.

The Tourer's engine was in a really sorry state with a connecting rod poking through the block, the camshaft was in two pieces and it had a broken sump and engine mounting. As my father was foreman of the machine shop at the local Albion Commercial Agency his spare engine was soon re-bored, crankshaft re-ground and bearings re-metalled. It was then re-assembled with new pistons (which I think came from Rover which lowered the compression) and fitted in the Gloria.

Several other areas of the Gloria needed attention so father made bushes and fitted oversize pins to repair the spring shackles, fitted new kingpins and bushes and switched around the seals in the tandem brake master cylinder which improved the braking efficiency. He also made front floorboards and seat mountings from some timber he had to hand.

The first run, after being granted an MoT by a tester who also owned a number of older cars, highlighted a problem with the clutch which would hardly grip once it was warm. One evening at around 6.00 pm we set about replacing the clutch by removing the floor, dropping the propshaft and pulling back the gearbox before fitting the spare clutch father had in stock. After refitting enough of the floor to save our feet from falling through we were out for a test run before 10.00 pm.

Father only used the Gloria occasionally on fine days in the summer for runs around the countryside. The left-hand photograph was taken of him at the wheel during one such occasion. After I had been driving for several years I also was allowed to take it out. By this time the engine had started to overheat after about five miles and the brakes were not what they should have been. Father was not keen on the idea of me taking it apart to rectify the problems, plus there certainly was not the same availability of spare parts compared with now.

I have now inherited father's Gloria which has been garaged since last licensed in 1988. There are several 'sore bits' that will need attention before presenting it for an MoT. Then I can once again enjoy open air motoring, having sold my Westfield kit car in 1999.

Richard Singer, Aberdeenshire

GLORIA TWELVE VITESSE FOURSOME DROPHEAD COUPÉ

Specification

Engine: 10.8 hp;
4 cylinders; 66 mm bore by
90 mm stroke; capacity
1,232 cc; overhead inlet and
side exhaust valve; twin
S.U. carburettors.
Gearbox: 4 forward speeds
and reverse with free-wheel
pre-selection.
Brakes: Lockheed
hydraulically operated on all
four wheels; handbrake
operating on rear drums.
Track: 4 ft. 2 in.
Wheelbase: 9 ft.
Production: August 1935 to
July 1937
Price New: £365

Our Gloria was originally owned by a whisky broker but she was then laid up during the war. My 'husband to be' Jack (a newly qualified solicitor), bought her in 1957 from another solicitor.

We had our first date in her when visiting Cambridge and it was then I found out about her habit of oiling plugs! When Jack was on national service in Debden, Essex, he would regularly drive up to Manchester to see me. On one such occasion it was so cold that Jack tucked his trousers into socks his to help keep out the draught from where the pedals came through the floor.

We were married on 16th April 1960 and took her on honeymoon to the Lake District. I then learnt to drive and passed my test in her. Later when our twin daughters were young I can clearly remember the sight of them standing on the back seat, with the roof down, with their long blonde hair and red ribbons blowing in the wind – you would not be allowed to do that on the road today!

After carrying the twins, our son and dog on many journeys we eventually replaced her as our everyday transport with a Jaguar 2.4 litre saloon. We were so attached to the Gloria that we did not sell her, but we gracefully retired her from daily transport to occasional runs and attending old car meetings.

Raie Lindsay, Glasgow

Featured Car

Registration Number:
AGB 413
Licensing Authority:
Glasgow
Registration Date:
November 1936
Notes: Six have been
recorded and two survive
with their original style
Cross & Ellis built
bodywork.
This car still exists in fine
condition.

Specification

Engine: 15.72 hp;
6 cylinders; 65 mm bore by
100 mm stroke; capacity
1,991 cc; overhead inlet and
side exhaust valves; single
S.U. carburettor.
Gearbox: 4 forward speeds
and reverse with free-wheel
pre-selection.
Brakes: Lockheed
hydraulically operated on all
four wheels; handbrake
operating on rear drums.
Track: 4 ft. 2 in.
Wheelbase: 9 ft. 8¹/₁₆ in.
Production: September
1935 to August 1936
Price New: £415

Featured Car

Registration Number:
CLL 365
Licensing Authority:
London
Registration Date:
January 1936
Notes: This is one of two
examples recorded and both
survive. This Gloria is
currently being restored.
The bodywork is by Cross &
Ellis coachbuilders and the
higher specification Gloria
Vitesse version was the most
expensive model, at £445,
that Triumph offered in
their 1935/6 model range.

I have always had a weakness for open cars, especially the foursome drophead coupé type, so when in 1966 I saw an advertisement for this Triumph in Sutton, Surrey, close to my then home in Banstead, I could not resist a look. I fell for the car immediately and bought it for the asking price of £15.

The seller, Eddie Pratt (pictured with the car) rented an old farm and stable building where he kept a number of interesting old cars (this was before Sutton was redeveloped). He was probably reducing his collection because his wife disapproved of his old car hobby and at his request our contacts had to be discreet. His wife, however, was quite happy for him to spend his evenings in a pub, so when he went to work on his cars this is where he said he was going. Before returning he would have a swig of beer so that he smelled appropriate for his arrival home!

In the event my purchase of the car was untimely since serious illness in my family, which had appeared to be on the mend, turned out not to be, and I found myself with no time or energy to devote to the car. Eddie and I kept in touch and when it became apparent that I would not have time in the foreseeable future to restore it he bought it back.

When I bought the car it was rather shabby and Eddie sent me this photograph some time after he had reacquired it, by which time he had clearly done quite a lot of work, at least cosmetically.

The car's coachwork was built by Cross & Ellis Ltd., and I clearly remember the coachbuilder's plate attached to the door sill bearing their 'CROSSLIS' trademark.

It was Eddie's understanding that the car had been originally ordered by the Hollywood star Merle Oberon who appeared in many 1930s films including playing the role of Cathy alongside Laurence Olivier and David Niven in the 1939 film *Wuthering Heights*.

I later lost contact with Eddie and I have no knowledge of the car after 1967, but I greatly regret my decision of not retaining it.

David Baker, Somerset

GLORIA SOUTHERN CROSS 2-SEATER

Specification

Engine: 10.8 hp;
4 cylinders; 66 mm bore by
90 mm stroke; capacity
1,232 cc; overhead inlet and
side exhaust valve; twin S.U.
carburettors.
Gearbox: 4 forward speeds
and reverse with free-wheel
pre-selection.
Brakes: Lockheed
hydraulically operated on all
four wheels; handbrake
operating on rear drums.
Track: 4 ft. 2 in.
Wheelbase: 8 ft.
Production: September
1935 to August 1937
Price New: £295

Featured Car

Registration Number:
Unknown
Licensing Authority:
Unknown
Registration Date:
1936
Notes: 24 have been
recorded and 13 survive
with their original style
bodywork.
Without knowing this
Gloria's registration number,
it cannot be confirmed
whether it is one of those
that survives.

This Triumph was purchased in 1936 or shortly afterwards by my father, Cuthbert Skinner, the fourth son of a very well known Skegness family, who were owners of the Sandbeck Hotel (on the sea front on the south-west corner of the clock tower) as well as a chain of butchers shops in this coastal town. Sadly the hotel was bombed by the Germans in 1941. It remained a bomb-site until the Sandbeck Amusement Arcade was built there in the 1960s.

This is the only picture I have of the Gloria. It is a sepia postcard-size photograph on which I have written on the back as a small child 'My Dad in his Triumph Gloria at Skegness' taken in 1940-ish.

'Cuth' (as father liked to be known) was, like the car he owned, good looking, full of fun, a true character and excellent company. He always loved two-seater sports cars and owned several over the years (despite being married with a family), including an MG and a 1949 Triumph Roadster, which I bought from him in 1957. Sadly his young life was ruined by the war due to the bombs and the evacuation of the citizens (and holiday makers) from Skegness, with the consequent loss of the family businesses.

He served in the Royal Air Force during the war but was invalided out in 1942 when a bomb fell off the bomb trolley whilst being loaded onto a Wellington bomber and crushed his foot. Thereafter he always walked with a stick but still managed to drive his beloved Gloria. Despite my arrival as an only child, he still continued with the car. I travelled on the shelf behind the seats! I can remember how cold and wet I got whenever the weather was bad. He was also a great social drinker and I spent many lunchtimes and evenings waiting in the Gloria while he was in the pub with my mother. I can well remember sitting in the Gloria (usually reading books if it wasn't dark) parked outside the officers' mess at RAF Newton in Nottinghamshire (Headquarters No.12 Group, Fighter Command) whilst he was socialising. I could often see them in the bar through the window. I don't know if this was by accident or design!

Gillian Dyer (née Skinner), Nottinghamshire

Specification

Engine: 10.8 hp;
4 cylinders; 66 mm bore by
90 mm stroke; capacity
1,232 cc; overhead inlet and
side exhaust valve; twin S.U.
carburettors.
Gearbox: 4 forward speeds
and reverse with free-wheel
pre-selection.
Brakes: Lockheed
hydraulically operated on all
four wheels; handbrake
operating on rear drums.
Track: 4 ft. 2 in.
Wheelbase: 8 ft.
Production: September
1935 to August 1937
Price New: £295

Featured Car

Registration Number:
CNB 180
Licensing Authority:
Manchester
Registration Date:
February 1936
Notes: 24 have been
recorded and 13 still exist
with their original style
bodywork.
This car still exists.

I remember that my husband, Stuart, purchased this Triumph in January 1955 from a garage in Barrow-in-Furness, Lancashire (now Cumbria). We spent many happy hours travelling around the country. My only unhappy recollection of the car was my first and only driving lesson – I never mastered the art of double de-clutching!

These photographs were taken with friends on the Honister Pass in the Lake District at Whitsuntide, 1955. Stuart can be seen behind the steering wheel and I am the brunette standing in the back of the Triumph.

In 1959, owing to family commitments, we reluctantly sold the Triumph to Neville Collier (*read his story on page 82*) who continued to cherish and enjoy it for a number of years.

Dorothy Ball, Warwickshire

GLORIA SOUTHERN CROSS 2-SEATER

I purchased my Gloria for £90 from Mr Stuart Ball in August 1959 and used it regularly until 1963 when it skidded on ice on a mountain road in North Wales. Unfortunately it hit a very solid stone wall, broke the chassis and bent the front axle, but no one was injured. Luckily two months later I saw a neglected Southern Cross for sale in London which I purchased. Over the next two years I rebuilt the Gloria using the chassis, front axle and various parts from the London car.

It was during this rebuild that I installed a 1,768 cc Lea Francis twin camshaft engine and gearbox and changed the back axle ratio to take the higher power output. I then drove the Gloria regularly again, touring all over Britain, until I sold it to Mr Bob Saunders in 1969.

The left-hand photograph was taken in either August 1961 or 1962 during our holiday. We had motored from Leamington Spa up to Black Cullins on the Isle of Skye for a week's climbing, but the weather was atrocious. After four days in the wind and rain we motored down to North Wales to some better weather. In total we covered about 1,000 miles and the Gloria never missed a beat.

The other photograph, taken in 1967, shows my mate tying his boot laces at the foot of Garbh Bheinn, west of Corran Ferry by Fort William, Scotland. Above the spare wheels was a luggage rack that I sometimes fitted to carry the extra winter camping equipment.

Neville Collier, Inverness-shire

Specification

Engine: 10.8 hp; 4 cylinders; 66 mm bore by 90 mm stroke; capacity 1,232 cc; overhead inlet and side exhaust valve; twin S.U. carburettors.
Gearbox: 4 forward speeds and reverse with free-wheel pre-selection.
Brakes: Lockheed hydraulically operated on all four wheels; handbrake operating on rear drums.
Track: 4 ft. 2 in.
Wheelbase: 8 ft.
Production: September 1935 to August 1937
Price New: £295

Featured Car

Registration Number: CNB 180
Licensing Authority: Manchester
Registration Date: February 1936
Notes: This car is currently in the USA and is now powered by Triumph's 1,767 cc engine. Installing this larger engine is popular with enthusiasts as it provides the car with the performance it can handle and deserves. Triumph did the same with at least two Gloria Southern Crosses (*see pages 85 & 86*).

Specification

Engine: 10.8 hp;
4 cylinders; 66 mm bore by
90 mm stroke; capacity
1,232 cc; overhead inlet and
side exhaust valve; twin S.U.
carburettors.
Gearbox: 4 forward speeds
and reverse with free-wheel
pre-selection.
Brakes: Lockheed
hydraulically operated on all
four wheels; handbrake
operating on rear drums.
Track: 4 ft. 2 in.
Wheelbase: 8 ft.
Production: September
1935 to August 1937
Price New: £295

Featured Car

Registration Number:
COG 645
Licensing Authority:
Birmingham
Registration Date:
July 1936
Notes: This second Gloria
Southern Cross model can
be identified from the
preceding year's model by
the standard fitment of
chrome stone guards to the
petrol tank sides.
This car still exists and is
currently being restored
with Triumph's later
1,767 cc overhead valve
engine.

GLORIA SOUTHERN CROSS 2-SEATER

When I was in my second year at university in 1961 I bought 'COG', a 1936 Gloria Southern Cross, from a fellow student, Adrian Moon for £40. Throughout the time at university she was often used for carrying unfeasibly large numbers of people to pubs and cricket matches, as well as being my removals van at the end of term.

In 1963 Kate and I were married and we set off from Chichester for our honeymoon in Cornwall. All was well until the last day when the gearbox dropped a bush, leaving top as the only functioning gear. I found that I could just get the car rolling in first gear before the cogs started slipping, so we managed to drive back to our flat in Wimbledon essentially in top gear all the way. Fortunately there was plenty of torque because she had been fitted with the larger Triumph 14/60 engine. The more difficult task was persuading our landlady that the gearbox was not going to go through the floor while two large South Africans and I rebuilt it in our kitchen.

'COG' remained our sole transport throughout a move to North London. With the birth of our son, we found that we could get him to sleep at night by putting him in his carrycot on the back bench seat and driving him round the streets of Kenton and Harrow. There were no rules about car seats in those days and this particular carrycot was of fibreboard and vinyl construction rather like a lidless picnic cold box.

Eventually after five years of use and many weekends spent under the car the time came to get something more reliable, so I bought a Hillman Imp. Enough said. 'COG' was consigned to the garage where she has been patiently awaiting restoration. The job is underway but has been badly interrupted by other priorities.

Tony Miles, Hampshire

GLORIA SOUTHERN CROSS 2-SEATER

Specification

Engine: 10.8 hp;
4 cylinders; 66 mm bore by
90 mm stroke; capacity
1,232 cc; overhead inlet and
side exhaust valve; twin S.U.
carburettors.
Gearbox: 4 forward speeds
and reverse with free-wheel
pre-selection.
Brakes: Lockheed
hydraulically operated on all
four wheels; handbrake
operating on rear drums.
Track: 4 ft. 2 in.
Wheelbase: 8 ft.
Production: September
1935 to August 1937
Price New: £295

This Southern Cross was at some time in its life fitted with a 1,767 cc Dolomite engine and gearbox in place
of the original Coventry Climax unit. I acquired it in exchange for a 1934 Gloria Ten Saloon, registered AVM
400, with a friend named Geoff Street when I lived in Sale, Cheshire.

The engine in the Southern Cross was found to do odd things to one of the spark plugs. The top of one of
the pistons had come off the skirt part, with only the engine's compression keeping the two parts together. If I
slowed down too quickly the piston top rose higher than usual and punched the spark plug gap shut! This
fault had arisen from the engine overheating due to the head gasket being fitted back to front, so closing off a
vital water passage. This Dolomite engine was an early pattern with a horizontal distributor, which
occasionally tried to throw its rotor arm off when I was cornering hard, doing no good to it or the distributor
cap.

With this more powerful than standard engine fitted it was ideal for towing. The caravan in the left-hand
photograph is my restored 1928 Eccles Jacobean 10 ft. Tourer that I acquired as a derelict rabbit hutch! It is
seen here with myself and my wife Dorothy on a journey to Devon to meet the car's designer, Walter
Belgrove, in August 1968. The second photograph, taken in 1969 by Dorothy's father, Jimmy Whittaker
(a retired wheelwright), shows my 1933 Winchester Light 15 caravan that I rescued from Kinver Edge in the
Midlands.

Glyn Lancaster Jones, Gwynedd

Featured Car

Registration Number:
DGF 864
Licensing Authority:
London
Registration Date:
August 1936
Notes: This car still exists
and is fitted with Triumph's
later 1,767 cc overhead
valve engine.

Specification

Engine: 13.95 hp;
4 cylinders; 75 mm bore by
100 mm stroke; capacity
1,767 cc; overhead valves;
twin S.U. carburettors.
Gearbox: 4 forward speeds
and reverse; synchromesh
gears to top, 3rd and 2nd.
Brakes: Lockheed
hydraulically operated on all
four wheels; handbrake
operating on rear drums.
Track: 4 ft. 2 in.
Wheelbase: 8 ft.
Production: December
1937
Price New: Not listed

Featured Car

Registration Number:
CKV 560
Licensing Authority:
Coventry
Registration Date:
December 1937
Notes: This Gloria Southern
Cross was built to special
order for J. P. Ferguson by
Triumph. The car's
commission plate reads 'SX
Special'. It differs to the
production model in having
the larger Triumph engine
instead of the Coventry
Climax designed engine.

GLORIA 14/60 SOUTHERN CROSS 2-SEATER

CKV 560 is an ex-works Special Southern Cross. It was built for J. P. Ferguson and fitted with a Dolomite G15 14/60 engine as original equipment. I have always understood that it was one of maybe four or five such cars, the others being built as high speed cars for Warwickshire police, although I have no proof of that.

First registered in December 1937 it remained in J. P. Ferguson's (Ferg) ownership until after the war. In about 1947 or '48 my father, Sidney Elgar, bought the car from his old friend. It was to become his business transport as well as the family car for the next 10 to 12 years. During that time it probably covered at least 250,000 mile, maybe more.

On Christmas day in 1949 or '50 my mother crashed the car near Hern Airport in snow and ice. It was written off and the wreck purchased by my father. With the insurance money he had the car rebuilt but with the body extended to make it a four-seater. The photographs show that the rebuild was successful!

Father competed with it in several Motor Cycling Club events but I don't know the extent of his competition driving at that time. The last time he and the car competed was the Land's End Trial in 1962 or '63. I navigated, aged 15 or 16, and we retired at Darracott hill, having grounded heavily on a rock ledge. The *Motor Sport* magazine reported:- 'S. Elgar's elderly Triumph graunched to a halt'. Ever after that event CKV 560 was known in the family as 'The Graunch'.

The left-hand photo was taken in either 1950 or '51 and shows me as a boy and my family at home, just after completion of our caravan, in Salisbury. CKV 560 was well capable of towing this home-made caravan which was based on an old Triumph Scorpion car chassis. The right-hand photo was taken of father competing in the 1953 MCC Exeter Trial.

The story of CKV 560, when owned by me, continues on the next page.

Ed Elgar, Hampshire

GLORIA 14/60 SOUTHERN CROSS 2-SEATER

Continued from the previous page.

In 1964 I left home in Wiltshire to start my engineering student apprenticeship in Coventry. CKV 560 went with me. I was now the third owner of the car. It wasn't a pretty sight, with bumps, bruises, rust and very tired rear springs showing the age of the car, after several years of neglect.

Despite its condition I ran the car very successfully through two student years before 'running' the big-ends on the M1 motorway by Watford Gap services. I had learnt to drive in this car (first solo aged about 14 on an airfield), as well as growing up with her, so she was very special to me. There now followed three years of rebuilding in various rented garages, with very little money, until June 1969 when the car emerged back onto the road. It was needed as the 'going-away car' for my wife and I after our wedding in July 1969.
CKV 560 was now back to a two-seater, as near in detail to her correct shape as I could manage at the time. Some of the materials used then would raise a few eyebrows, but it worked, and the car looked good. The photographs show me during the 'restoration' phase and the finished result. The engine had been fully refurbished and I still have the bill for £91 14s 5d.

We only ran the car for just over a year before family increase loomed, so it came off the road in 1970 and has not been driven since. Not wishing to see it gradually deteriorate further and knowing that I cannot devote time for another restoration I made the hard decision in 2006 to sell it. The good news is that a Triumph enthusiast (who owns a similarly engined Dolomite) has bought it and intends to return it to the condition this historically important car deserves.

Ed Elgar, Hampshire

Specification

Engine: 13.95 hp; 4 cylinders; 75 mm bore by 100 mm stroke; capacity 1,767 cc; overhead valves; twin S.U. carburettors.
Gearbox: 4 forward speeds and reverse; synchromesh gears to top, 3rd and 2nd.
Brakes: Lockheed hydraulically operated on all four wheels; handbrake operating on rear drums.
Track: 4 ft. 2 in.
Wheelbase: 8 ft.
Production: December 1937
Price New: Not listed

Featured Car

Registration Number: CKV 560
Licensing Authority: Coventry
Registration Date: December 1937
Notes: Two have been recorded and both survive. It is thought that Triumph may not have built more than a handful of these larger engined Gloria Southern Crosses. No publicity literature has been discovered for this model, suggesting that it was not marketed to the general public. This car is due to be restored soon.

Specification

Engine: 13.95 hp;
4 cylinders; 75 mm bore by
100 mm stroke; capacity
1,767 cc; overhead valves;
twin S.U. carburettors.
Gearbox: 4 forward speeds
and reverse; synchromesh
gears to top, 3rd and 2nd.
Brakes: Lockheed
hydraulically operated on
all four wheels; handbrake
operating on rear drums.
Track: 4 ft. 2 in.
Wheelbase: 9 ft.
Production: September
1936 to August 1938
Price New: £318

Featured Car

Registration Number:
ADA 819
Licensing Authority:
Wolverhampton
Registration Date:
October 1936
Notes: 115 have been
recorded and 13 survive
with their original style
bodywork.
This car no longer exists.

VITESSE 14/60 SALOON

My father, one of five brothers, was born at Yewtree Farm on the A5 road near Stafford. He remembered my grandfather letting the cows out to graze beside this road and a biplane landing on the road for the pilot to ask for directions. Wow, how times have changed!

With little work on the farm during the Great Depression, father learnt butchery and then opened a successful butcher's shop on Colway Road in Wolverhampton. Within a few years he could afford to change his motorbike for a car. Father visited his local Triumph dealer's showroom to test drive a silver Vitesse he admired. After a drive in this demonstrator he agreed to buy a new Vitesse in the same colour and arranged to collect it direct from the Triumph factory.

Carrying a tin of running-in oil, father travelled to the factory on the back of his brother-in-law's motorbike. On arrival father examined a silver Vitesse parked and awaiting collection, which he initially thought was his. Without saying who he was, father asked to see the manager and then asked him: "How many cars do you make with the same engine and chassis numbers?" The manager answered: "None sir." "Well, this car has the same numbers as a Wolverhampton dealer's demonstrator." The manager then replied "You are correct; this is the car you refer to. It was returned to us for a new speedometer and a paintwork touch-up, and is now ready for a customer to collect. Why do you ask?" "Well, I am that customer, but I have ordered a new car not this used example. I was warned about this dealer and the tricks he was up to so I wrote down the numbers to make sure that I collected a new car." "You will have a brand new car," replied the manager. Father collected it a few weeks later!

In 1947 father returned to farming and bought Hurst Farm (where I was born the following year) less than two miles from Yewtree Farm. Proud of his cars he only rarely let my sister drive them. On one occasion, not wanting to damage the Vitesse while driving through the farm gateway, she opened both gates to allow plenty of room and drove through the middle of the gap, forgetting the raised centre gate stop which proceeded to rip off the battery tray as she drove over it!

I would love to end this story by saying that I now drive a pre-war Triumph, but instead I drive the next best thing; a 1935 Crossley Regis powered by a 1,122 cc Coventry Climax engine.

Harvey Bould, Staffordshire

VITESSE 14/60 SALOON

Specification

Engine: 13.95 hp; 4 cylinders; 75 mm bore by 100 mm stroke; capacity 1,767 cc; overhead valves; twin S.U. carburettors.
Gearbox: 4 forward speeds and reverse; synchromesh gears to top, 3rd and 2nd.
Brakes: Lockheed hydraulically operated on all four wheels; handbrake operating on rear drums.
Track: 4 ft. 2 in.
Wheelbase: 9 ft.
Production: September 1936 to August 1938
Price New: £318

I bought this Vitesse in 1954, then only an unbelievable 17 years old. She was hand painted in a sort of baked bean colour and the recorded mileage was 37,000 which I didn't consider correct owing to the car's poor condition. The mascot was missing but later a friend gave me an Alvis eagle which graced the radiator and was still fitted when I sold the car.

The first photograph was taken on a caravanning holiday near Canterbury in 1955 and the other was taken in the late 1960s.

A non-drip paint called 'Jelly-Pex' came on the market in the late 1950s, so armed with this product I changed the colour to cherry red.

Several things went wrong over the years but I managed to sort them one way or another. The most difficult was a cracked engine block which I replaced, after a lot of searching, with a Dolomite engine plus a gearbox from a local scrapyard for £5. It was soon installed in the car, but it failed to start. A farmer friend came with his tractor and even towing her it failed to start despite a huge amount of back firing which frightened everyone and everything in sight! Comparing the two engines we discovered that on the original the distributor was mounted near the top of the engine, but on the 1938 Dolomite engine it was mounted on the side and the rotor arm rotated the opposite way. We swapped the plug leads around and away the engine went.

After about 30 years it was decided that the 'old girl' must go and she was sold to Mr Noble of Leicester. When he collected her she was running, just! I drove her onto the trailer feeling a little sad as she had been part of the family for so long. I decided to follow in a 1951 Armstrong-Siddeley Whitley almost to Derby and then watched her disappear into the misty July evening. Mr Noble restored her and when completed he drove her back for me to see. She was as new, or even better; a truly noble achievement!

Robert Clarke, Derbyshire

Featured Car

Registration Number: RC 4864
Licensing Authority: Derby
Registration Date: March 1937
Notes: It is the view of many Triumph enthusiasts that the Vitesse 14/60 was the best saloon Triumph produced. Its sporting lines were matched by the fine performance of their all new overhead valve engine. This car still exists in fine restored condition.

Specification

Engine: 13.95 hp;
4 cylinders; 75 mm bore by
100 mm stroke; capacity
1,767 cc; overhead valves;
twin S.U. carburettors.
Gearbox: 4 forward speeds
and reverse; synchromesh
gears to top, 3rd and 2nd.
Brakes: Lockheed
hydraulically operated on
all four wheels; handbrake
operating on rear drums.
Track: 4 ft. 2 in.
Wheelbase: 9 ft.
Production: September
1936 to August 1938
Price New: £318

Featured Car

Registration Number:
DAF 721
Licensing Authority:
Cornwall
Registration Date:
April 1937
Notes: Vitesses can be
identified from the earlier
and very similar Gloria
Vitesses by its deep front
wings (which now extend
below the front bumper)
and the slightly more
rounded radiator surround.
This car no longer exists.

VITESSE 14/60 SALOON

I bought DAF 721 in 1956 from a second-hand car site in Hull to use as an everyday car. After a few weeks use it was obvious all was not well with the engine and other features. On one occasion on the way to work I had to stop and flap the front doors about to disperse the smoke and fumes inside the car. That evening I said to my father "I'll have to get rid of it". His reply was to the effect that this was a silly move and advised me to take it to his garage and tell them to put it right. They did this for £75 – half the price I had paid for the car. This transformed the car which I then enjoyed using for work and touring Yorkshire (pictured in the right-hand photograph) for several years. With hindsight, I suspect that the dealer had doctored the engine with "Piston Seal", a proprietary remedy for worn out engines. The left-hand photograph pictures me jumping out of the Vitesse on my parents' drive.

During this time I learned a lot about mending and coping with old cars. As is common with wood framed bodies, it did show cracks at the boot top corners and above the windscreen framing.

After selling the Vitesse in 1960 for £50, I was saddened to hear that its new owner had overturned the car and written it off.

I thought, during my custody of the car, that the Vintage Sports Car Club was misguided in not accepting the Vitesse as a 'post vintage thoroughbred' because I am sure it was a far superior model to many of their coveted specimens. I understand that in 2007 they recognised the error of their ways and have now accepted them along with all the other pre-war Triumph models. Nonetheless, one tends to look back now through rose-tinted spectacles; was it really as good as I thought?

Having fond memories of the Vitesse, I bought an earlier Gloria to restore in 1978. Unfortunately when finished it didn't live up to my old Vitesse and I eventually exchanged it for a 1936 MG sports car.

Norman Wilkinson, East Yorkshire

VITESSE 2-LITRE SALOON

I bought this Vitesse in 1958 when I was 19 years old. It had been stored in a large barn in the grounds of Hatfield House and I immediately fell in love with this low slung car. It was painted two tone grey with gleaming chrome headlights, red leather interior and fitted with Ace wheel discs. It was important that my then fiancée, Gerry (we married in 1960), gave her approval, so I picked her up on my motorcycle and when she saw the car her feelings were the same as mine, so a purchase was forthcoming. The car was being offered for the princely sum of £60, but this was beyond my means so I had to approach my boss who loaned me the money which I repaid at £10 a month.

Over the winter months the Vitesse was kept outside so I decided to cover it with a large tarpaulin and then place an oil burning sump heater underneath the engine. This usually turned out to be a vain effort in making the engine easier to start the following morning!

Fuel consumption was rather heavy and I thought a pair of new SU carburettors might help. With very little spare money available my dear Gerry stepped in and 'donated' her holiday money so that for £8 they were purchased and fitted. I think that the fuel consumption remained the same!

This photograph of Gerry and me, taken in 1959, is the only one I have where my Vitesse features. The bonnet is up and I am making an adjustment to one of the headlamps. In the background is my future father-in-law's brand new Ford Popular.

Once while waiting in the middle of the A1 Great North Road, ready to turn right into Welwyn Garden City, the back of the Vitesse was hit by a removal lorry and a large amount of damage was caused to the rear near-side. The lorry owners', Bullens I think, denied responsibility but the AA successfully fought my case and it was repaired at no cost to me. I only had 'third party' insurance cover and I believe the repair cost was more than I paid for the Vitesse.

I can still recall the lovely gentle hiss of the twin SUs and the exhilarating feeling of driving at speeds over 50 mph with that lovely long bonnet way out in front! Sadly, and unwisely, the car was sold after a couple of years as I was about to enter the forces and fuel economy was to become important.

Peter Kibblewhite, Norfolk

Specification

Engine: 15.72 hp; 6 cylinders; 65 mm bore by 100 mm stroke; capacity 1,991 cc; overhead valves; twin S.U. carburettors.
Gearbox: 4 forward speeds and reverse; synchromesh gears to top, 3rd and 2nd.
Brakes: Lockheed hydraulically operated on all four wheels; handbrake operating on rear drums.
Track: 4 ft. 2 in.
Wheelbase: 9 ft. 8 1/16 in.
Production: September 1936 to August 1938
Price New: £338

Featured Car

Registration Number: DLA 895
Licensing Authority: London
Registration Date: December 1936
Notes: 38 have been recorded and eight survive with their original style bodywork.
This car no longer exists.

Specification

Engine: 15.72 hp;
6 cylinders; 65 mm bore by
100 mm stroke; capacity
1,991 cc; overhead valves;
twin S.U. carburettors.
Gearbox: 4 forward speeds
and reverse; synchromesh
gears to top, 3rd and 2nd.
Brakes: Lockheed
hydraulically operated on
all four wheels; handbrake
operating on rear drums.
Track: 4 ft. 2 in.
Wheelbase: 9 ft. 8¹/₁₆ in.
Production: September
1936 to August 1938
Price New: £338

Featured Car

Registration Number:
EOE 407
Licensing Authority:
Birmingham
Registration Date:
May 1938
Notes: This car was seen at
club events in the mid-
1970s. Due to its
deteriorating ash frame,
which allowed the doors to
burst open when driven, it
was taken off the road soon
after. It was last reported as
being in a poor dismantled
condition.

VITESSE 2-LITRE SALOON

This maroon Vitesse was purchased in 1946 by Denis Rayner of Harbourne, Birmingham, who subsequently owned it for nearly 30 years. He bought it from the first owner, whose identity is unknown.

Pleased with the performance of his Vitesse, Denis built a large caravan soon after, as can be seen in the right-hand photograph. During his Vitesse ownership he always commented on how well and smoothly it ran by comparison with other cars he had.

In the late 1940s Denis purchased another Vitesse, which presumably had suffered badly during the war, and dismantled it for spares; no details are known of this car except it was black.

Denis was a great enthusiast for the Swift motorcycle (like myself and that is how we met and became friends) and the left-hand photograph shows him, holding the microphone, with the Triumph at the Swift Owners Club's rally at Evesham in September 1960.

In April 1972 Denis advertised his Vitesse in the Pre-1940 Triumph Owners Club's newsletter. It read: "1938 2-Litre Vitesse Saloon in very good condition, running & either MoT or capable of same, complete with a lorryload of appropriate spares including axles etc. £350." The newsletter's editor went on to say: "I have seen this car and have heard it running – very smooth. Some work needs to be done on it, but only of a minor nature. Mr Rayner has been running this car since the war with only short spells off the road. It is finished in plum, with the original beige upholstery. I have only seen one other car so original, and including the spares, think that this would be a worthwhile buy."

Andrew Marfell, Warwickshire

VITESSE 2-LITRE SALOON (converted to a Tourer)

It was August 1961 while at home on holiday in South Wales when I first saw this lovely car. It had its hood down and was being driven by an old school friend. He stopped and I admired the car which he said he wished to sell. Expressing an interest and on hearing that it had been fitted with a new hood we agreed on £120 and the Vitesse was mine. What a difference this car was to the Austin A40 in which I had just passed my test!

The first of many experiences with it was my struggle to balance the worn twin carburettors. Having heard of a specialist in Cardiff, I made an appointment to have them overhauled. A short while later when driving over the infamous Newport Bridge, pre-M4, the mechanical carburettor linkage jammed on full throttle causing traffic problems and much embarrassment. A friendly lorry driver came to my aid and relocated the linkage.

The following Easter, driving in the Gloucester area, an ominous engine rattle started together with the loss of oil pressure. My RAC guide indicated that luckily there was a repair specialist fairly near and on arrival two men in the yard could not fail to hear my approach. They looked up and did the usual teeth sucking and head shaking and diagnosed what I had feared, a big end bearing had failed. This required stripping down the engine and re-white metalling the bearing. When tested after the rebuild the oil pressure was fluctuating from normal to zero, so another strip down was needed and the problem was found. The small key drive to the oil pump had sheared and was slipping so causing loss of pressure. This was replaced but I was only charged the original cost of £35 for the initial work – true enthusiasts!

Following marriage and purchase of a family car, the Vitesse was stored in a nearby private garage. Stupidly, over the winter, having forgotten to drain the radiator or add antifreeze, I found to my horror that a small rectangular piece had blown from the side of the engine block. This necessitated drilling and tapping a replacement cover over the hole.

The Vitesse continued to be used during summers until 1967. By then I had joined the Royal Navy and was due to go to sea so it was reluctantly sold on to a fellow officer.

Farewell Vitesse and thank you for an interesting, informative and enjoyable period of ownership. I understand that you are still in existence, residing in Italy. We may meet again one of these days, who knows!!!

Peter Newman, Hampshire

Specification

Engine: 15.72 hp; 6 cylinders; 65 mm bore by 100 mm stroke; capacity 1,991 cc; overhead valves; twin S.U. carburettors.
Gearbox: 4 forward speeds and reverse; synchromesh gears to top, 3rd and 2nd.
Brakes: Lockheed hydraulically operated on all four wheels; handbrake operating on rear drums.
Track: 4 ft. 2 in.
Wheelbase: 9 ft. 8$^{1}/_{16}$ in.
Production: September 1936 to August 1938
Price New: £338

Featured Car

Registration Number: PGP 320
Licensing Authority: London
Registration Date: August 1954
Notes: This 1937 Vitesse started life as a saloon, as illustrated below, and was rebuilt probably in 1954 (when it was re-registered PGP 320) with this one-off tourer body. Its original registration is not known. This car still survives in fine condition in Italy and is often mistaken for a Gloria Southern Cross.

Engine: 15.72 hp;
6 cylinders; 65 mm bore by
100 mm stroke; capacity
1,991 cc; overhead valves;
twin S.U. carburettors.
Gearbox: 4 forward speeds
and reverse; synchromesh
gears to top, 3rd and 2nd.
Brakes: Lockheed
hydraulically operated on all
four wheels; handbrake
operating on rear drums.
Track: 4 ft. 4 in.
Wheelbase: 9 ft. 8¹/₁₆ in.
Production: September to
December 1936
Price New: £368

Featured Car

Registration Number:
Unknown
Licensing Authority:
Unknown
Registration Date:
1936 or 1937
Notes: 22 have been
recorded and four survive
with their original style
bodywork. These
Continentals are identical
to the Dolomite 2-Litre
Saloons apart from being
fitted with the Vitesse style
radiator grille. This was to
cater for the more
conservative customer.
It is thought that this car no
longer exists.

CONTINENTAL 2-LITRE SALOON

In the late 1930s my father, Harry, sold his 1934 Armstrong-Siddeley and bought a Triumph Continental. He was a trained engineer and used it throughout the war years maintaining it himself as spares were in short supply during that period. He had a well equipped workshop with a lathe, milling machine etc. and was skilled in pattern making, casting, hardening, tempering and machine work. He could also weld, braze and solder and passed some of these skills on to me and my brother.

When war had broken out my father had joined his father's company of building and civil engineering contractors but retained his engineering skills. During the war the company was engaged mainly in repair and rebuilding of war damaged property, mostly via War Office contracts. They also built and repaired furnaces in the steel works. Army camps and runways for the air force were also part of the new work undertaken. With all this essential war work my father was allowed to continue to drive his Continental.

My father was in his early forties by this time and during the run-up to D-Day he volunteered for service in the Naval Reserve and spent some time as 'Engineer' on an MFV (Motor Fishing Vessel) running supplies from Portsmouth to the Isle of Wight from which the invasion was sprung. He was invalided home in late 1944 after being catapulted into moving machinery when a mine exploded nearby and was discharged after it was found that he had a fairly serious heart condition. He was also a Section Commander in the Special Constabulary.

I remember the Continental as being a cross between a Vitesse and a Dolomite, having the Vitesse's radiator grille and the Dolomite's body. It was very good looking and reliable. My outings in the car were mainly restricted to the occasional journeys to school and accompanying my father to construction sites. One other journey that lives in my memory was over the Yorkshire Moors to Whitby in 1946. There was snow lying on the high ground and with no heater it was very cold! After the war my father sold the Continental and treated himself to a new car, a Ford Pilot, in about 1949.

This Continental must have left me with a favourable impression, because in 1956 I bought a 1949 Triumph Roadster and then keeping faithful to the Triumph marque I bought a new Herald Coupé around 1959, but this gave me a lot of trouble and rusted away very quickly!

Brian Beeden, Norfolk

DOLOMITE 14/60 SALOON

Specification

Engine: 13.95 hp;
4 cylinders; 75 mm bore by
100 mm stroke; capacity
1,767 cc; overhead valves;
twin S.U. carburettors.
Gearbox: 4 forward speeds
and reverse; synchromesh
gears to top, 3rd and 2nd.
Brakes: Lockheed
hydraulically operated on all
four wheels; handbrake
operating on rear drums.
Track: 4 ft. 4 in.
Wheelbase: 9 ft.
Production: August 1936 to
January 1937
Price New: £338

Featured Car

Registration Number:
EEH 29
Licensing Authority:
Stoke-on-Trent
Registration Date:
Between January and
March 1937
Notes: 17 have been
recorded and it is thought
that none survive with their
original style bodywork.
This first and short lived
Dolomite model housed its
spare wheel below the boot
floor. All subsequent
4-cylinder Dolomites had
their spare wheel mounted
on the boot lid.
This car no longer exists.

The owner of this Dolomite was my grandfather, Alphonse Joseph, a truly remarkable man. A Belgian refugee who arrived in this country in 1916 aged 14, he immediately started work in a munitions factory at Richmond in Surrey. Obviously a quick learner, he soon progressed to become an expert machinist and skilled engineer.

After the end of the First World War, Alphonse apparently got involved with motor racing and claimed to have test driven Bentleys at Brooklands during the 1920s and 1930s. He also changed jobs during this period and went to the Beverley Works at Barnes, a company which produced metal forgings and then, at the outbreak of World War Two, switched to munitions.

It is believed that these photographs were taken in Richmond Park around 1940. In the right-hand photograph Alphonse can be seen standing proudly next to his Dolomite. It has all the regulation blackout equipment in place at the front of the car, including masked sidelights and bulb removed from its offside headlamp, but he has not painted the wing and running board edges white as recommended. It is not known how long he kept the car or what happened to it.

By the end of the war he was an experienced design engineer. Following a short stint in France helping to rebuild the arsenal at St.-Étienne, he went to work at Sun Engineering in Kingston, Surrey. It was there that he began to develop fire fighting systems and equipment, a process he continued at a company called Fire Armour Ltd.

In the late 1940s or early 1950s, Alphonse joined commercial vehicle coachbuilders James Whitson & Co. Ltd. of West Drayton in Middlesex. In addition to coaches and lorries, Whitson also manufactured fire engines (including some of the famous Green Goddess pump units) and Alphonse was appointed manager of the Whitson Anti-Fire Appliance & Equipment Co. Ltd. While working at Whitson, he took out no less than five UK patents concerning foam generating equipment and special valves for fire fighting use (other patents were registered in the USA).

Sadly, Alphonse began to suffer from ill health in 1961 and then had to give up work altogether. He died in November 1965.

I wish to thank my parents, Arthur and Juliette Davis, for helping me with information about my grandfather and finding these photographs.

Suzanne Davis, Surrey

Specification

Engine: 15.72 hp;
6 cylinders; 65 mm bore by
100 mm stroke; capacity
1,991 cc; overhead valves;
twin S.U. carburettors.
Gearbox: 4 forward speeds
and reverse; synchromesh
gears to top, 3rd and 2nd.
Brakes: Lockheed
hydraulically operated on all
four wheels; handbrake
operating on rear drums.
Track: 4 ft. 4 in.
Wheelbase: 9 ft. 8¹/₁₆ in.
Production: January to
April 1937
Price New: £388

Featured Car

Registration Number:
CHP 179
Licensing Authority:
Coventry
Registration Date:
March 1937
Notes: Dolomites were
designed by Triumph's chief
stylist Walter Belgrove and
this particular car is
mentioned in his papers
Three have been recorded
with the original vertical
louvred bonnet and one
survives with its original
style bodywork.
This car was last licensed on
24th March 1958 and no
longer exists.

DOLOMITE 2-LITRE SALOON DE LUXE

My sister Jane and I have conferred and can recollect that this car was purchased by our father in 1937. It was bought direct from Coventry where it was previously used as a factory demonstrator. It was painted maroon and had a beige leather interior. These photographs were taken of me with the car soon after dad's purchase. The first photograph was taken at my mother's family home in Harpole, Northamptonshire, and the others were taken at father's farm in Preston Deanery also in Northamptonshire.

Dad used the car regularly until the war when in 1940 it was stored in our garage on blocks until 1946. It was then brought out again for regular use. I clearly remember dad working on the car with it up on jacks and the front off-side wheel removed. Looking at its large flanged brake drum (being a young boy, I did not know what it was) I suggested to my father, who was looking a little flustered, "If you take off the other wheels you could drive it on the railway lines." He was not amused!

After the war I was a boarder at Park House School in Paignton, Devon, and can remember many journeys to Paddington railway station in London to catch the train along with other pupils and a school master. Two journeys particularly stand out: one when the car suffered a front near-side tyre blow-out whilst travelling along the A5 just north of Dunstable in Bedfordshire and the other when I painfully left the skin of my top lip on the top edge of the dashboard after dad braked hard to avoid a dog.

About 1951 dad bought a Ford Zephyr Six and sold the Dolomite to a business acquaintance, Wilfred Green from Kettering, Northamptonshire. I understand, from the Pre-1940 Triumph Owners Club's archives that Wilfred kept the Dolomite until 1958 when it was scrapped. Jane remembered that dad remarked that the car was sold for double the amount he had paid for it. Not so these days!

Patrick Castell, Buckinghamshire

DOLOMITE 14/60 SALOON DE LUXE

Specification

Engine: 13.95 hp;
4 cylinders; 75 mm bore by
100 mm stroke; capacity
1,767 cc; overhead valves;
twin S.U. carburettors.
Gearbox: 4 forward speeds
and reverse; synchromesh
gears to top, 3rd and 2nd.
Brakes: Lockheed
hydraulically operated on all
four wheels; handbrake
operating on rear drums.
Track: 4 ft. 4 in.
Wheelbase: 9 ft.
Production: July 1937 to
July 1938
Price New: £348

Featured Car

Registration Number:
EGT 292
Licensing Authority:
London
Registration Date:
August 1937
Notes: This Dolomite
model was the first to have
the chevrons on the bonnet
sides, but interestingly this
car is fitted with the Art
Deco styled bird mascot that
had by this time been
replaced with the Vitesse
winged lady.
This car no longer exists.

Around 1961, when whatever banger I was driving at the time had expired, I went to Ken Seaton's car breakers yard just outside Ashford, Kent. He had two runners on offer: an MG J2 and a Dolomite both at £14. It looked like it was going to rain and the MG's hood was in tatters, so I plumped for the Dolomite.

The Dolomite was surprisingly sound, the main problems being two cracks where the windscreen pillars join the scuttle, holes in the back door skins made by the front doors as a result of failed straps and a previous owner having painted the body with something that looked liked tar.

I decided the car was worth rescuing and started to use it as my daily transport, but it was not an easy relationship as lots of annoying little mechanical faults surfaced. The rockers had been starved of oil at some time and the cup of one pushrod had worn through. The splines stripped on one of the rear hubs and worst of all the water pump kept collapsing.

During the winter of 1961/2 I had many problems with snow blowing into the engine bay while the car was parked outside my place of work. I had the bright idea of putting a sack over the engine but I forgot to remove it before driving home. The smell of burning soon became apparent, and I thought that it was caused by lack of water (it had a radiator leak), so called in to a garage in the centre of Ashford to top up the radiator. Lifting the bonnet, flames from the burning sack shot to the heaven and pandemonium reigned with garage staff rushing to find fire extinguishers etc. I extinguished my eyebrows and grabbed an armful of snow and threw it onto the engine. This had the desired effect but the garage staff were not amused and told me in no uncertain terms to clear off! 500 yards down the road the draught re-ignited the smouldering bulkhead insulation so another armful of snow was needed! I examined the damage upon arriving home and found that apart from the insulation having been burnt from the HT leads it was otherwise okay.

I loved the car and soldiered on with it for about six months when its life was terminated by another car pulling out into the side of me as I was driving down Tenterden High Street.

These days it would be considered a small job to replace the running board and rear wing but in 1961 it was considered terminal. The photo shows the car after it had been standing for a few months after the accident.

I have not completely lost touch with pre-war Triumphs as I have grafted a Gloria remote gearchange unit to my Reliant engined Austin Seven special that I currently own.

Don Munnings, Kent

Specification

Engine: 13.95 hp; 4 cylinders; 75 mm bore by 100 mm stroke; capacity 1,767 cc; overhead valves; twin S.U. carburettors.

Gearbox: 4 forward speeds and reverse; synchromesh gears to top, 3rd and 2nd.

Brakes: Lockheed hydraulically operated on all four wheels; handbrake operating on rear drums.

Track: 4 ft. 4 in.

Wheelbase: 9 ft.

Production: July 1937 to July 1938

Price New: £348

Featured Car

Registration Number: BSC 659

Licensing Authority: Edinburgh

Registration Date: November 1937

Notes: 141 have been recorded and six survive with their original style bodywork.

This car no longer exists.

DOLOMITE 14/60 SALOON DE LUXE

This photograph of me standing proudly beside my Dolomite was taken in 1960 or '61. At the time I was a poorly paid teacher, living in Bournemouth and working in Poole. I soon got tired of travelling by bus and looked around for a cheap car. By sheer luck I met a Dolomite enthusiast who had two of them for sale. I bought the cheaper one for £40.

My wife Lyn and I quickly fell in love with 'Dolly' from her waterfall grille to the walnut dash and leather seats – somewhat shabby though they were. She could still give many newer cars a run for their money, even though she was then almost 25 years old. As you might expect, she needed some work – work I could ill-afford on my teacher's salary, so it became a DIY project. I fibreglassed the radiator's header tank, filled holes and dents with Bondo, and hand-painted her in Valspar green. On one occasion my enthusiastic friend and I replaced the crown wheel and pinion in the street with Dolly propped up against the kerb in rather undignified fashion on her two nearside wheels! It gave us so much pleasure owning her and was a delight as we drove all over southern England in modest elegance.

The Consuls and Victors of the time were like tawdry women of the street compared to her stately carriage and pre-war quality. Sadly, when Lyn and I moved to Canada in 1961 we had to sell her. No one wanted to buy her. I ended up giving her away for £14 to a local garage owner. Somehow I felt I had betrayed her. Since then I have owned a number of desirable cars – a brand new Sunbeam Rapier, a Triumph GT6, and a Sunbeam Alpine among them, but I really would trade them all to have Dolly back.

Harry Seddon, Vancouver, Canada

DOLOMITE 14/60 SALOON DE LUXE

Specification

Engine: 13.95 hp;
4 cylinders; 75 mm bore by
100 mm stroke; capacity
1,767 cc; overhead valves;
twin S.U. carburettors.
Gearbox: 4 forward speeds
and reverse; synchromesh
gears to top, 3rd and 2nd.
Brakes: Lockheed
hydraulically operated on all
four wheels; handbrake
operating on rear drums.
Track: 4 ft. 4 in.
Wheelbase: 9 ft.
Production: July 1937 to
July 1938
Price New: £348

Featured Car

Registration Number:
EWB 273
Licensing Authority:
Sheffield
Registration Date:
November 1937
Notes: Although Gerry's
photos are blurred, the
much smaller headlights can
still be seen. They look
smaller than the trumpet
horns!
This car no longer exists.

June 22nd 1957. My nineteenth birthday and a planned climbing holiday in Scotland with three pals just about four weeks away. We needed a car. Our local car lot had a 1937 Triumph Dolomite on the forecourt – what a birthday present to myself.

The fact that it had two, four inch diameter ex-W.D. lorry headlamps mounted where big chrome Lucas lamps should be, did not matter.

On went the roof rack, up went the rucksacks, on went the 'L' plates, fixed to front and rear bumper with big rubber bands, and off we set for Fort William.

We never made it. Thanks to the dim ex-W.D. headlamps, somewhere near Carlisle in the middle of the night we ran off the road and demolished a line of tubular steel fencing. The engine, having stopped, wouldn't restart; there was no power in the batteries. Out came the trusty starting handle and she started first turn. We reversed off the fence, did a damage assessment, and found that the sum total of damage was that the front 'L' plate had fallen off. It was never replaced!

We had noticed that there always was a battery problem with four people in the car. However, we did get as far as Luss on Loch Lomond where Baz and I met two girls who we took out one night for a romantic drive through the glens. True to form, as soon as it went dark and we put the lights on, the engine stopped. That cost us a fortune in taxi fares and even more in damaged egos to find out that the insulation on the steel battery covers had worn out, and every time anyone sat on the back seat the covers shorted out the batteries.

Happy days, and there were so many more in that wonderful old Dolomite.

Gerry Smith, Yorkshire

Specification

Engine: 13.95 hp;
4 cylinders; 75 mm bore by
100 mm stroke; capacity
1,767 cc; overhead valves;
twin S.U. carburettors.
Gearbox: 4 forward speeds
and reverse; synchromesh
gears to top, 3rd and 2nd.
Brakes: Lockheed
hydraulically operated on all
four wheels; handbrake
operating on rear drums.
Track: 4 ft. 4 in.
Wheelbase: 9 ft.
Production: July 1937 to
July 1938
Price New: £348

Featured Car

Registration Number:
GPC 10
Licensing Authority:
Surrey
Registration Date:
December 1937
Notes: This car no longer
exists.

DOLOMITE 14/60 SALOON DE LUXE

I was introduced to my Dolomite GCP 10 by a business friend as my previous car (a Flying Standard 12) had to be replaced due to brake problems. This happened around 1952. Its front so attracted me with its chrome twin headlamps and horns and its radiator grille with its flying lady that I could not resist it. It became known as 'Eagle's Flying Lady' both at RAF Biggin Hill and BOAC at Heathrow Airport. The original log book contained photos of its winning history when in 1938 it won three races as a Triumph works race entry.

It gave me great service, particularly during a three month spell when I commuted between Heathrow and Bisham Waltham. Never below 60 mph, it did the 60 mile trip in 60 minutes, a journey that would take over two hours today with modern speed limits and volumes of traffic.

During its life I had to recheck its engine tappet clearances and tune the twin carbs every week but it was a wonderful car with its wooden veneer interior panelling and red leather upholstery. It was wonderful to drive with good steering and ran very smoothly with plenty of power. Eventually wear and tear created stress cracks around the rear boot door access and front wings and costly specialist aluminium welding repairs would be needed and so she had to go, much to my regret.

The next time I saw GPC 10 I was travelling home from RAF Biggin Hill through Coulsdon. The new owner had painted the front wings a shocking brown but the cracks were still in the boot access surround and the poor engine sounded terrible to me.

The photo is of my wife with GPC 10 outside my father-in-law's country pub in White Waltham in 1953. It was a lovely car even by today's standards.

Arthur Eagle, Berkshire

DOLOMITE 14/60 SALOON DE LUXE

Specification

Engine: 13.95 hp;
4 cylinders; 75 mm bore by
100 mm stroke; capacity
1,767 cc; overhead valves;
twin S.U. carburettors.
Gearbox: 4 forward speeds
and reverse; synchromesh
gears to top, 3rd and 2nd.
Brakes: Lockheed
hydraulically operated on all
four wheels; handbrake
operating on rear drums.
Track: 4 ft. 4 in.
Wheelbase: 9 ft.
Production: July 1937 to
July 1938
Price New: £348

Featured Car

Registration Number:
BKY 419
Licensing Authority:
Bradford
Registration Date:
1937
Notes: This car no longer
exists.

This Dolomite was the fourth car that my parents had owned. The first was a 1934 Wolseley Hornet Special bought in 1944 and the second car was a Vauxhall 14. My parents were in business at that time and it was thought that the Vauxhall fitted their image better. The third car was a pre-war Ford V8 which is what I learned to drive in, passing my test in 1953. In 1954 the V8 was replaced by BKY 419, a very swish looking car of the time, purchased from Reg Timms Motors in Luton. It was finished in black cellulose on the outside with a very nice interior with brown leather upholstery, a wooden dashboard to house the instruments and it smelled like a proper car inside.

These photographs taken by brother Stuart in 1954 are from a family holiday spent touring the south coast. One is of my parents, George and Hilda Wilson and my sister Hazel on the beach with the Dolomite in the background. The other one is of me doing a bit of maintenance during the tour. (Note the rear hinged suicide doors front and rear).

Occasionally I was allowed to borrow the 'Dolly' to take out my girlfriend of the time as it always made a good impression. By that time my personal transport was a 1932 Eustace Watkins Wolseley Hornet Special, not the sort of device to impress the ladies, so if a new girlfriend was on the horizon I had to speak nicely to mum and dad to borrow the Dolomite. My main memory of the car, apart from its elegant looks and a very nice engine, was that compared with most other cars of the time, it would corner very well.

My parents were both car enthusiasts and appreciated the sleek lines of the Dolomite. It was bought as the family car and only used for family days out at the weekend and for holidays etc. Dad didn't have to use it to go to work so it rarely went out during the week. It was always garaged and I remember that my father would never put it away wet and we always had to dry it off first. Polishing was a weekly ritual. All three offspring have completed a Dolomite grille polishing apprenticeship!

In 1956 the Dolomite was exchanged for a 4-litre Austin Sheerline saloon in silver grey over black, again via Reg Timms Motors.

Arthur Wilson, Buckinghamshire

Specification

Engine: 13.95 hp;
4 cylinders; 75 mm bore by
100 mm stroke; capacity
1,767 cc; overhead valves;
twin S.U. carburettors.
Gearbox: 4 forward speeds
and reverse; synchromesh
gears to top, 3rd and 2nd.
Brakes: Lockheed
hydraulically operated on all
four wheels; handbrake
operating on rear drums.
Track: 4 ft. 4 in.
Wheelbase: 9 ft.
Production: July 1937 to
July 1938
Price New: £348

Featured Car

Registration Number:
FGF 362
Licensing Authority:
London
Registration Date:
August 1938
Notes: This car no longer
exists.

DOLOMITE 14/60 SALOON DE LUXE

After demob, my husband Peter and I decided a trip through France to Switzerland would shake off wartime blues and give our Dolomite a good run after being holed up in the garage for so many years. It was silver with huge trumpet horns on the front operated by a rocker switch on the steering wheel, which went from soft to loud. Woe betide anyone who stood too close when the loud side was pressed!

The year was 1948 (when the above photo of us was taken). Peter had served in the Royal Engineers and I in the FANYs. We left our home town Caterham at the crack of dawn for Dover. Passing through a sleepy Kent village, Peter spotted an MG sports car parked in a lay-by. As we passed he shouted: "Tally Ho! Competition" and put his foot down hard on the accelerator. We were soon pursued by the MG, which turned out to be a police car, and the elated occupants gave Peter a speeding ticket!

Joining the ferry, our Dolomite had to be craned from the dockside (as shown in the other photo) and plonked on the tiny ship's deck, which could only accommodate about four cars. The crossing was extremely rough and I feared that our Dolomite, which was not secured in any way, might be swept overboard, but all was well when we arrived at Calais.

Our Dolomite created interest wherever we stopped. We found that Northern France was more war-torn than the south and reconstruction had barely begun. Toilets were primitive and unhygienic, we preferred to seek a secluded patch of woodland. Switzerland, by contrast, was clean and breathtakingly beautiful, with everything in plentiful supply. We stayed in Lucerne before returning to Calais. It was late afternoon and the last ferry of the day had sailed when we arrived back at Calais, so we booked in to a small hotel in Wimereux. The proprietor showed us to our room and proudly pointed to the wardrobe, explaining that the holes that peppered it had been made by German bullets! Next morning we caught the ferry back home and reflected on our enjoyable breakdown free holiday.

After this holiday we soon traded our Dolomite for a Triumph Renown which was a beautiful car but not the crowd stopper that the Dolomite had been.

Joyce Osborn, Gloucestershire

DOLOMITE 1½-LITRE SPECIAL SALOON

Specification

Engine: 13.95 hp;
4 cylinders; 75 mm bore by
100 mm stroke; capacity
1,767 cc; overhead valves;
twin S.U. carburettors.
Gearbox: 4 forward speeds
and reverse; synchromesh
gears to top, 3rd and 2nd.
Brakes: Lockheed
hydraulically operated on all
four wheels; handbrake
operating on rear drums.
Track: 4 ft. 4 in.
Wheelbase: 9 ft.
Production: December
1937 to August 1939
Price New: £328

Featured Car

Registration Number:
CNX 466
Licensing Authority:
Warwickshire
Registration Date:
August 1938
Notes: Based on the
narrower Vitesse style
chassis the 1½-Litre was the
smallest of the Dolomite
saloons. 50 of these
Dolomites fitted with the
larger 1,767 cc engine have
been recorded and four
survive with their original
style bodywork.
This car no longer exists.

In Summer 1957 I was a Technical Cadet at the RAF Technical College, Henlow on leave and needing a new set of wheels to replace a game but tame pre-war Standard 10. In the local paper, the *Stratford-upon-Avon Herald*, there was an advert for a 1937 Triumph Dolomite and my father, who sold cars for a local garage, sent me off to have a look. When I went back to him he asked what the registration number was and I informed him that it was CNX 466. He went to his desk and got out a record of sales book and he said, "Oh yes, I sold that new to Fred Winter in 1937" and he showed me the entry. Fred Winter ran a large drapery store in Stratford and he had passed the car on to his son during the war.

I bought the car, if I remember, for £120 and I had to return to College in Bedfordshire a couple of days later. Of course I wanted to travel back in it to show off my rather smart car to my fellow Cadets as there were only a few of us that could afford a car. When we looked under the bonnet there was a very crude tin sheet made from a beaten out five gallon drum, across the top of the engine. We removed this and the following evening I set off for Henlow at the end of my leave.

My route involved going up Sunrising Hill on the road to Banbury and half way up there was a loud bang and clouds of steam. I lifted the bonnet and torch light showed filthy water everywhere as the radiator cap had blown off. So that was why there had been a cover over the engine! I knew that there was a big house at the top of the hill so I set off, leaving the car parked, and knocked on a big imposing front door. When I explained my problem, the astonished owner kindly leant me a big enamelled jug full of water which I used to fill the radiator. I started the car, returned the jug and made my way to college, at a fairly slow speed to avoid boiling again.

The most important reason for owning a car was to transport myself and friends to Bedford where there was a ladies' teacher training college and we had a social life to pursue. As one of the few car owners, and with three seats available, I was quite popular and soon met the lady whom I eventually married a couple of years later.

We still had the Dolomite when we got married and went off on our honeymoon from South Wales to Cornwall but we suffered a large number of punctures and Hilary became quite adept in setting up the jack and helping me change the wheels.

We sold the Dolomite in 1960 not long before we were posted to Malta and really did feel sad as that car served us well and had been an important part of our first years together and had many stories to tell.

Michael Evans, Hampshire

Specification

Engine: 13.95 hp;
4 cylinders; 75 mm bore by
100 mm stroke; capacity
1,767 cc; overhead valves;
twin S.U. carburettors.

Gearbox: 4 forward speeds
and reverse; synchromesh
gears to top, 3rd and 2nd.

Brakes: Lockheed
hydraulically operated on all
four wheels; handbrake
operating on rear drums.

Track: 4 ft. 4 in.

Wheelbase: 9 ft.

Production: December
1937 to August 1938

Price New: £328

Featured Car

Registration Number:
ELJ 422

Licensing Authority:
Bournemouth

Registration Date:
September 1938

Notes: Even though
Triumph increased the
engine capacity from 1,496
to 1,767 cc they confusingly
continued to call this
Dolomite a '1¹/₂-Litre' with
'Special' added to its name.
This car still exists in
excellent restored
condition.

I have owned 'Old Dollie' since 1965. Its first owner was Mrs Florence Oddie from Bournemouth. It had done 27,000 miles from new when I bought it and was basically to the original factory specification but Solex carburettors were fitted instead of the advertised SU's.

In 1965 petrol was about 4s 6d (22¹/₂p) a gallon and the best the car would do was 24 miles per gallon. I used the car for everyday transport for the next four years. I remember going over a hump-backed bridge with four passengers in the car when suddenly the car was full of smoke and sparks. The batteries had shorted-out on the floor pans much to the alarm of my back-seat passengers.

The photograph shows me standing next to Old Dollie when parked at Brandon Hall Hotel, Coventry, in the summer of 1967.

I decided to restore the car in 1982 when the appropriate funds were released by my wife. The body is aluminium and is held on the chassis by four bolts. It was removed by lifting it off with a length of wood placed across my shoulders, head through the sunshine roof and my wife pulling the chassis out of the garage whilst I tiptoed through the chassis members. I then gently lowered the body onto carefully placed piles of bricks. Some of the ash frame was replaced, the engine re-bored, new wiring fitted, the body re-painted and then all reassembled.

My son, Tom, was born in 1988 and his first trip in Old Dollie was from hospital in December with many hot water bottles on the back seat. The gynaecologist was an 'old car' enthusiast and insisted on a trip round the hospital grounds before he would discharge my wife and son!

Old Dollie has been up the Prescott hillclimb, round most of the race tracks in the UK and also on the MIRA and Millbrook proving grounds. It has also attended many weddings, often receiving more attention than the bride. Today it is still driven on a regular basis and can often be seen pottering around my local lanes.

Bob Morley, Leicestershire

DOLOMITE 14/60 SALOON

This photograph shows my father, Harold Kirkby Avill, standing outside his home in Doncaster with the Dolomite he owned between 1956 and 1958.

The Dolomite had been owned by the family before father had it, as his brother, Charles Smithson Avill, bought it about 1952. Uncle Charlie lived in Kinnerton Street Mews, London. Living next door was Gilbert Harding the newspaper correspondent and famous television panellist on the *What's My Line?* television quiz show. Uncle Charlie was regularly called upon to help Gilbert out of a taxi when he returned home worse for wear from drink! Uncle Charlie was chauffeur to Lady Fermoy, a close friend of the Queen Mother, and his wife Stella was nanny to her children.

After about three years of ownership Uncle Charlie sold his Dolomite to my brother Howard who kept it for six months before passing it on to father.

Unfortunately it was eventually scrapped after its chassis had broken.

Lance Smithson Avill, Yorkshire

Specification

Engine: 13.95 hp; 4 cylinders; 75 mm bore by 100 mm stroke; capacity 1,767 cc; overhead valves; twin S.U. carburettors.
Gearbox: 4 forward speeds and reverse; synchromesh gears to top, 3rd and 2nd.
Brakes: Lockheed hydraulically operated on all four wheels; handbrake operating on rear drums.
Track: 4 ft. 4½ in.
Wheelbase: 9 ft. 2 in.
Production: September 1938 to August 1939
Price New: £348

Featured Car

Registration Number: HPB 830
Licensing Authority: Surrey
Registration Date: Between September and November 1938
Notes: Changes for this third and last version of the Dolomite 14/60 Saloon included flush fitting doors, glass louvres above the door windows and larger boot. 84 have been recorded and seven survive with their original style bodywork. This car no longer exists.

Specification

Engine: 13.95 hp;
4 cylinders; 75 mm bore by
100 mm stroke; capacity
1,767 cc; overhead valves;
twin S.U. carburettors.
Gearbox: 4 forward speeds
and reverse; synchromesh
gears to top, 3rd and 2nd.
Brakes: Lockheed
hydraulically operated on all
four wheels; handbrake
operating on rear drums.
Track: 4 ft. 4 in.
Wheelbase: 9 ft.
Production: August 1938 to
September 1939
Price New: £298

Featured Car

Registration Number:
FHT 952
Licensing Authority:
Bristol
Registration Date:
October 1938
Notes: 45 of these
Dolomites have been
recorded and three survive
with their original style
bodywork. These later Sport
Saloons can be
distinguished from the
Special Saloons by their
wider grille and the front
side lights being raised to the
top of the front wings.
This car no longer exists.

This Dolomite was my first car. I bought it in 1957 from a national service guy in Muswell Hill, North London. I think that it cost about £25 which I thought was good value but it turned out to be a 'basket case'.

The first long journey undertaken was from Tottenham to South Shields for the purpose of letting my parents visit a relative. This was an overnight trip starting at 8 pm and arriving at 8 am. The fuel and oil consumption were equal as the car laid down a smoke trail which a destroyer would have been proud of! It dawned on me that something in the engine needed attention. Having no mechanical knowledge, I enlisted a friend who new a man etc. The engine came out and when the pistons were removed no piston rings could be found, except for broken bits in the sump! The engine was rebuilt, after a fashion, giving me a couple of years use.

I was driving home from work one evening when the propshaft fell off. The passenger in the front was a very large lady who wanted to know what had happened. What could I say? I didn't know. We pushed the car to the curb, my passengers walked home and I looked underneath and decided it was a job for the AA!

These photos were taken at Winchester Cathedral on the journey down to our Cornish holiday. We arrived at Newquay and the following day was spent surfing. After a day's rest the 'Dolly' would not budge. We tried to release the brakes with no success, so it was another call to the AA. They found that the brakes had glued on as a result from the hub bearings' grease overheating and leaking onto the brake shoes. With all the steep hills encountered, everything had got too hot.

I attended evening classes three times a week at Enfield Technical College and I gave my friend Alan a lift. On two occasions problems with Dolly were rife. The first was when we approached the T-junction in White Hart Lane. The lights turned red and I applied the mighty brakes which worked much to my surprise and my equally surprised passenger lurched forward and went through the floor! A little later the same traffic lights were changing to amber/green so I put my foot down hard. Dolly shuddered forward and Alan lurched backwards as his seat's back snapped!

I eventually sold Dolly to a friend for £10 with a fiver down and the balance when he could afford it. Needless to say I only received £5. During a cold spell the engine block cracked and so ended the life of my first Dolomite.

Alan Davis, Buckinghamshire

DOLOMITE 14/60 FOURSOME DROPHEAD COUPÉ

Specification

Engine: 13.95 hp;
4 cylinders; 75 mm bore by
100 mm stroke; capacity
1,767 cc; overhead valves;
twin S.U. carburettors.
Gearbox: 4 forward speeds
and reverse; synchromesh
gears to top, 3rd and 2nd.
Brakes: Lockheed
hydraulically operated on all
four wheels; handbrake
operating on rear drums.
Track: 4 ft. 4½ in.
Wheelbase: 9 ft. 2 in.
Production: Early 1938 to
September 1939
Price New: £388

Featured Car

Registration Number:
GR 6798
Licensing Authority:
Sunderland
Registration Date:
June 1939
Notes: This car's Tickford
body was built by Salmon &
Sons. 16 have been
recorded and three survive
with their original style
bodywork.
This car still survives, in fine
condition, in mainland
Europe.

During the summer of 1971, I was displaying my 1948 Daimler DB18 Barker Drophead Coupé at Durham County Show when a young music student asked me if I knew of anyone who might be interested in buying either of the two cars owned by his aged violin teacher. They were a 1934 Morris 10/6 Doctors Coupé and a Dolomite convertible. I already knew how handsome the Dolomite was as a 2-Litre Roadster attended local old car meetings, so I was careful not to tell anyone else of this find before I had bought the Dolomite for £240!

I suspect that this Dolomite had been repainted gun metal grey judging from the quality of the finish. Traces of dark blue paint were found which I guessed was its original colour. The leather upholstery was also blue. The rear double seat squab had an inflatable inner cushion, but it had perished and deflated! The radio, apparently fitted from new, still worked.

This Dolomite's only previous owner was the music teacher's brother and it had been garaged since his death quite some years earlier. The music teacher was very keen to show me the refilling point for the brake fluid which was behind tandem cylinders under the floor. His concern was understandable as it required refilling in a couple of days as all the hoses were perished and the optimistic wrappings of electricians tape could not staunch the fluid loss!

The sale of my wife's Fiat 500D had part financed the purchase, so the Dolomite became Betty's everyday car, quite a change for her! These photos of the Dolomite outside our home were taken in 1972.

Not long after I'd carried out some work on the Dolomite, I received a telephone call from Betty; she had arrived at work to find oil pouring out of the chrome bonnet louvres. Happily it was not as dire as it first seemed, as petrol from the banjo joint to the float chambers had squirted onto the inside of the bonnet and washed off several years of old oil deposits!

After a few years of great fun with the Dolomite it was taken off the road for a major restoration, but I never completed it, so after nearly 18 years ownership it was sold in 1989. A proud subsequent owner told me that the car had been restored and painted 'magnolia', which struck me as being a bit lavatorial! I would like to have seen it painted blue over black wings. In 1996 I read that it was sold at auction for £15,600.

John Wilkie, Tyne & Wear

Specification

Engine: 13.95 hp;
4 cylinders; 75 mm bore by
100 mm stroke; capacity
1,767 cc; overhead valves;
twin S.U. carburettors.
Gearbox: 4 forward speeds
and reverse; synchromesh
gears to top, 3rd and 2nd.
Brakes: Lockheed
hydraulically operated on all
four wheels; handbrake
operating on rear drums.
Track: 4 ft. 4½ in.
Wheelbase: 9 ft. 2 in.
Production: September
1938 to August 1939
Price New: £375

Featured Car

Registration Number:
ECV 788
Licensing Authority:
Cornwall
Registration Date:
September or October 1938
Notes: Compared with the
standard saloon the Royal's
body is two inches wider
with a similar difference in
height. All other
specifications are the same.
The larger body was claimed
to allow five adults to be
seated in greater comfort.
This car no longer exists.

DOLOMITE 14/60 ROYAL SALOON

My first love was a 650cc Triumph Thunderbird motorcycle and it served me very well. At the time I was in the Royal Navy and it was soon a case of 'have ship, must travel' so the bike went to a new owner. Upon my return to the UK in 1953 I bought what I consider to have been my best car ever, this black Dolomite with its beige leather upholstery, luxurious pile carpets and beautiful waterfall grille. The left-hand photograph shows me sitting on the bumper.

One of the things that I remember most about the car is not its speed or style but the simple, yet very efficient, window mechanism on the driver's door. It was just a big chrome lever you raised to close the window and pushed down to lower. It was so easy that it must have had balancing weights to compensate for the weight of the glass. The imposing twin trumpet horns were operated by a 'Soft' and 'Loud' rocker switch mounted on the steering wheel boss. If you rocked the switch towards 'Soft' the horns would emit just a short blast, but rock towards 'Loud' and they sounded like the trumpet section of the Royal Marines Band!

I was living at St Austell and based temporarily in the Royal Naval Barracks in Devonport. I did the 40 mile journey most weekends crossing the Tamar via the Torpoint ferry (there was no bridge at Saltash then). I used to enjoy swinging the Dolomite through some of the lovely bends on the old A38. Of course traffic was very light in those days and you certainly could not do it today! A problem I did encounter with the car was its reluctance to start on very damp misty mornings.

I was a young petty officer and the time came for me to do overseas service again so unfortunately the Dolomite had to go and sadly I have not seen or heard of it since. Several years later I met Lieutenant Commander Ashthorpe, who also owned a Dolomite, and he told me that he remembers mine and regretted that he did not buy it as his was a bit worse for wear!

In more recent times I have owned four post-war Triumph saloons and I am still a keen enthusiast of the marque.

Ron Bray, Devon

DOLOMITE 14/60 ROYAL SALOON

My father bought this Dolomite new and collected it from the factory in Coventry during May 1939. I understand that it was just before Triumph was put into the hands of the receivers. The Dolomite proved to be comfortable and reliable transport for the family. Father was fond of the car and when it was time to change it for something more modern he decided to pass it on to me rather than sell it to a stranger. In the mid-1950s I learnt to drive and passed my test in the Dolomite.

I remember going to Silverstone to see the British Grand Prix with my friends in the car. To gain a better vantage point to view the racing we built a stand around the car. It was constructed from beer crates and had the provision to safely store our refreshments!

A couple of years after passing my driving test I had the unfortunate experience of rolling the Dolomite into a ditch! The left-hand photograph shows me sitting on the bonnet with an L-plate displayed. This had been tied on the bumper by my friends as a joke! The right-hand photo clearly shows the filler I applied to repair the bodywork.

On another occasion I had decided to seek my fortune! I left Kettering via my sister who lived in Norfolk. However, the Dolomite blew a piston and I spent the next month or so waiting for a replacement part. I never did seek my fortune and came back to Kettering where I have lived ever since.

Like my father, I could not bring myself to sell the Dolomite so it is still with me, stored safely in its garage. Hopefully I will get round to restoring it to its former glory.

Arnold Reeves, Northamptonshire

Specification

Engine: 13.95 hp; 4 cylinders; 75 mm bore by 100 mm stroke; capacity 1,767 cc; overhead valves; twin S.U. carburettors.
Gearbox: 4 forward speeds and reverse; synchromesh gears to top, 3rd and 2nd.
Brakes: Lockheed hydraulically operated on all four wheels; handbrake operating on rear drums.
Track: 4 ft. 4$\frac{1}{2}$ in.
Wheelbase: 9 ft. 2 in.
Production: September 1938 to August 1939
Price New: £375

Featured Car

Registration Number: ARP 785
Licensing Authority: Northamptonshire
Registration Date: May 1939
Notes: 32 have been recorded and four survive with their original style bodywork.
This car still exists and awaits restoration.

Specification

Engine: 13.95 hp;
4 cylinders; 75 mm bore by
100 mm stroke; capacity
1,767 cc; overhead valves;
twin S.U. carburettors.
Gearbox: 4 forward speeds
and reverse; synchromesh
gears to top, 3rd and 2nd.
Brakes: Lockheed
hydraulically operated on all
four wheels; handbrake
operating on rear drums.
Track: 4 ft. 4½ in.
Wheelbase: 9 ft. 2 in.
Production: September
1938 to August 1939
Price New: £375

Featured Car

Registration Number:
FXP 260
Licensing Authority:
London
Registration Date:
June 1939
Notes: This car still exists
and awaits restoration.

DOLOMITE 14/60 ROYAL SALOON

I bought this Dolomite in April 1971. I saw her sitting in the yard of a filling station near Chichester with a faded 'For Sale' sign in the windscreen. I had seen a Dolomite only once before in the late 1950s and I still remember, as a small boy, thinking what a superb looking car it was. Now I felt that excitement again as I looked at this brash yet dignified beauty.

The proprietor of the garage was selling her for someone nearby who wanted £95 which was more than a month's wages for a young apprentice like me. I didn't argue and paid the man £5 deposit and returned again a fortnight later with the balance, most of which was borrowed from my father. Although she had obviously been static for some while she started first time on the button and so commenced five years of grand and eventful motoring.

In 1972 I was asked to bring the car to my local British Leyland dealer for the *Alton Gazette's* photo-shoot and article to compare it with the 'new' Triumph Dolomite. The left-hand photo was taken and shows the manager, I think his name was Bill Collier, with me to his right.

I shudder to remember how I treated her then although, in those days, she was regarded as little more than a banger, albeit a rather fine one. I was a reckless youth and used her as a tractor and a battering ram. I drove her across ditches, through hedges, over fields and up river beds. We had 'how many people can we get in a Dolomite (and drive to the pub) parties' and I was once paced at just over 70 mph, six up, going around the Winchester by-pass. I also have a vague recollection of causing frowns of consternation among older members of the Pre-1940 Triumph Owners Club at an early 1970s rally when I nearly turned her over while negotiating the cones in the driving test! Despite all this and with the very barest of maintenance she never let me down during the many thousands of miles travelled. However the fun ended abruptly one very cold winter's night in 1976 when I left her outside without draining the block and radiator. She froze solid and the water jacket blanking plate at the rear of the block was forced off complete with the surrounding casting. Since then she has sat under cover at the various locations around the country to which my career has taken me.

I have now settled in rural Somerset and perhaps one day I will start restoring her.

Adrian Stephens, Somerset

DOLOMITE 1½-LITRE ROADSTER COUPÉ

Specification

Engine: 11.81 hp; 4 cylinders; 69 mm bore by 100 mm stroke; capacity 1,496 cc; overhead valves; twin S.U. carburettors.
Gearbox: 4 forward speeds and reverse; synchromesh gears to top, 3rd and 2nd.
Brakes: Lockheed hydraulically operated on all four wheels; handbrake operating on rear drums.
Track: 4 ft. 4 in.
Wheelbase: 9 ft.
Production: April 1938 to July 1938
Price New: £348

After selling my Gloria (*see page 54*) I purchased this Dolomite Roadster. I would like to mention at this point that I cannot remember how much I paid for either cars or how much I sold them for, but it was probably in the region of £50 to £100. Strangely though I do have the receipt and original log book for my very first car, a 1932 Morris Eight tourer for which I paid £12 10s on 2nd October 1957 when I was aged 18. Incidentally, Road Tax was then also £12 10s per annum!

Back to the Dolomite. It was painted red and silver and these photographs feature my girlfriend of the time and myself sitting in the car, with its roof down, on a warm sunny day. They were taken in the car park of a pub along the Enfield Ridgeway. I thought that it was a superb looking vehicle, lovely to drive and having the benefit of a dickey seat which was a great feature. I would love to own this model today if I could find one at a reasonable price.

I would add that since then I have owned many classic cars including an MG J2, early Jaguar E Type Roadster, Ford 289 Mustang, Mach 1 Mustang, Sunbeam Talbot 90, Daimler V8 250, Lotus Cortina Mk1, Daimler Conquest, Citroën Light 15 and Corvette Stingray.

A year after writing the above Graham Shipman contacted me to say that the following information on this Dolomite had been discovered from Doncaster's car registration archives: Martyn Richardson, the last registered owner, had this car for a year before handing it to R. J. Bloomfield (car breakers) in Alexandra Road, Ponders End on 15th October 1960. Coincidentally at this time Graham's grandfather, Arthur Shipman, was running the family business Ashby's Plating Works, located in the same street as R. J. Bloomfield!

Eric Whitehouse, Cornwall

Featured Car

Registration Number: ADT 264
Licensing Authority: Doncaster
Registration Date: July, 1938
Notes: Six have been recorded and two survive with their original style bodywork. Both survivors are now fitted with Triumph's 1,767cc engine, as it is recognised that this model was under powered with its original 1½-litre engine.
This car no longer exists.

Specification

Engine: 13.95 hp;
4 cylinders; 75 mm bore by
100 mm stroke; capacity
1,767 cc; overhead valves;
twin S.U. carburettors.
Gearbox: 4 forward speeds
and reverse; synchromesh
gears to top, 3rd and 2nd.
Brakes: Lockheed
hydraulically operated on all
four wheels; handbrake
operating on rear drums.
Track: 4 ft. 4 in.
Wheelbase: 9 ft.
Production: April 1938 to
1940
Price New: £395

Featured Car

Registration Number:
XG 6142
Licensing Authority:
Middlesbrough
Registration Date:
1938
Notes: The other Dolomite
featured in the right-hand
photo is a 1937 Dolomite
14/60 Saloon de Luxe. Its
EGW 207 registration
indicates that it was
originally registered in
London.
These cars no longer exist.

DOLOMITE 14/65 ROADSTER COUPÉ

George Salter established his King's Arms Garage business in Summertown, Oxford, during the 1930s and his son, Ronald, joined him after his national service in the 1950s. It was at this time, while serving my apprenticeship at the nearby Ford main dealer, that I would cycle past the King's Arms Garage on my way to work each morning and on my return journey home. Two cars I can clearly remember seeing, displayed in their forecourt, were this pair of Dolomites: one was an ivory saloon and the other was a green roadster. These distinctive cars were an unusual sight and I was fascinated to find out more about them. My opportunity arose soon after I had bought my Triumph Gloria Six Saloon. I was rebuilding its engine and remembering the Triumph connection I visited the garage to see if they could supply me with a pushrod. Fortunately they helped find a replacement and I got the chance to speak to them about the Dolomites.

Many years passed and after recently completing the build of my 1938 Dolomite two-seater special, I started to wonder whatever happened to those two Dolomites. To satisfy my curiosity I made attempts to contact anyone with knowledge of the garage or the cars, but without success. Then quite unexpectedly a friend brought me into contact with Ronald Salter and to my joy not only did he remember these cars, but showed me these photos. The photograph of the saloon and roadster was just how I remembered them parked side by side all those years ago. The other photo shows the roadster minus its headlamps with Ronald sitting proudly behind its steering wheel.

Ronald told me that the Dolomites probably met an early demise, as did many other pre-war cars, when the MoT was introduced. The garage business however went from strength to strength taking on an agency for Rootes cars.

Derry Aust, Oxfordshire

DOLOMITE 14/65 ROADSTER COUPÉ

When Fisher, my husband, bought this Dolomite in 1950 its bodywork was painted pale green. He later had it resprayed white and arranged the fitting of a new hood. His interest in cars came from his father who used to race Bugattis at Brooklands between the wars. Fisher enjoyed entering this car into concours d'élégance events and with some success too, winning the Brighton and Eastbourne events. The left-hand photograph was taken during the 1951 Brighton concours and the right-hand photograph during the Eastbourne concours in the Devonshire Park Ballroom. The lady pictured with Fisher and the car was a friend of ours, who had taken my place during these two concours events as I was expecting our first child.

We travelled in the Dolomite all over Europe, usually with me relegated to the dickey seat when travelling with friends! One of the plausible reasons, explained to me by Fisher, for travelling 'second class' was to shift the weight balance when a spring had broken while driving through France. To do this I had to swap my comfortable front seat for the 'dickey' with Fisher's well built friend who was accompanying us!

Eventually we had to sell it and buy a more suitable family car when children started to appear! Fisher sold it to the film and theatre actor Laurence Naismith (remembered well for his role as captain of the doomed Titanic in the 1958 British award winning epic *A Night To Remember* which also starred Kenneth More).

After the Dolomite was sold we did see it once more at Brooklands during a rally organised for cars of its vintage. Looking back I feel that it is a shame that we sold the car, as it would have been good to have kept it along with many other possessions sold over the years.

During the period of our Dolomite ownership we also had for a time a 14/60 Vitesse Saloon which Fisher used. On one occasion, when he was in the Fleet Air Arm stationed at Lee-on-the-Solent in Hampshire, and with no available petrol, Fisher filled its tank with aviation fuel. I cannot remember now, but I imagine the Vitesse performed better than ever with this fuel on board!

Pauline Cruttenden, East Sussex

Specification

Engine: 13.95 hp; 4 cylinders; 75 mm bore by 100 mm stroke; capacity 1,767 cc; overhead valves; twin S.U. carburettors.
Gearbox: 4 forward speeds and reverse; synchromesh gears to top, 3rd and 2nd.
Brakes: Lockheed hydraulically operated on all four wheels; handbrake operating on rear drums.
Track: 4 ft. 4 in.
Wheelbase: 9 ft.
Production: April 1938 to 1940
Price New: £395

Featured Car

Registration Number: DFS 131
Licensing Authority: Edinburgh
Registration Date: August 1939
Notes: 48 have been recorded and 13 survive with their original style bodywork. Unfortunately this car, which was so well looked after until the late 1950s, has not survived.

Specification

Engine: 15.72 hp;
6 cylinders; 65 mm bore by
100 mm stroke; capacity
1,991 cc; overhead valves;
triple S.U. carburettors.
Gearbox: 4 forward speeds
and reverse; synchromesh
gears to top, 3rd and 2nd.
Brakes: Lockheed
hydraulically operated on all
four wheels; handbrake
operating on rear drums.
Track: 4 ft. 4 in.
Wheelbase: 9 ft. 8 in.
Production: April 1938 to
1940
Price New: £450

Featured Car

Registration Number:
DDD 375
Licensing Authority:
Gloustershire
Registration Date:
August or September 1938
Notes: 20 of these elegant
Roadsters have been
recorded and eight still
exist. All the survivors are
in fine restored condition.
This car no longer exists.

DOLOMITE 2-LITRE ROADSTER COUPÉ

This Dolomite was owned by my father, William Turnbull. Apparently this photograph on the left was taken out of the window of the furnished room in Dartmouth Road, Willesden, were my parents lived after they were married.

My father's recollection is that he bought the Dolomite in the 1950s for £100 in London when he came out of the Army. Although it had been laid up, it fetched a good price because it was difficult to buy new cars at that time as the majority were going for export.

Father remembers it as a lovely fast car but a hassle if he wanted to charge the batteries, as the only way of accessing them was by removing the dickey seat and the floorboards. It ran well and took them on a holiday to Gloucestershire (by coincidence this is where the Dolomite was originally registered). He owned the car for about five years after which he sold it to a car breakers yard in Neasden! This is where the trail of DDD 375 may have ended. At that time everyone wanted new cars which were available again in the home market.

Some years later father was watching the 1945 film *Blithe Spirit*, starring Rex Harrison, Constance Cummings, Kay Hammond and Margaret Rutherford, and he was surprised when he spotted that Rex Harrison's car was DDD 375 (as illustrated in the right-hand photograph). As it was a light two-tone colour he did not immediately recognise it as his Dolomite. It was painted black when he owned it. Perhaps if father had known that it had been the 'star' of this film he would not have sent it off to the scrapyard!

Neil Turnbull, Essex

DOLOMITE 2-LITRE ROADSTER COUPÉ

Specification

Engine: 15.72 hp;
6 cylinders; 65 mm bore by
100 mm stroke; capacity
1,991 cc; overhead valves;
triple S.U. carburettors.
Gearbox: 4 forward speeds
and reverse; synchromesh
gears to top, 3rd and 2nd.
Brakes: Lockheed
hydraulically operated on all
four wheels; handbrake
operating on rear drums.
Track: 4 ft. 4 in.
Wheelbase: 9 ft. 8 in.
Production: April 1938 to
1940
Price New: £450

Featured Car

Registration Number:
DKV 536
Licensing Authority:
Coventry
Registration Date:
January 1939
Notes: This car survives in
fine roadworthy condition.
Its first registered owner was
the Triumph Company Ltd.

I traded in my Monte Carlo (*see page 39*) for this magnificent Dolomite in the early 1950s. It was for sale at Raymond Way Motors in Kilburn, a firm not noted for dealing in quality cars, but they assured me that it had been the personal property of the boss even though not registered in his name. The day I came to collect it I parked my Monte Carlo nearby and gave the keys to the firm's rep. When he got in to drive it to the garage it resolutely refused to start and had to be towed away!

I had always admired the lines of the Dolomite Roadster and before the war I desperately tried to persuade my father to buy one but being more practically minded than myself he chose a 2-Litre Saloon model instead.

I was now the proud owner of the car I had coveted for many years and it looked splendid with its Ace wheel discs and the contrast of the black paintwork against the masses of chrome. It was used as daily transport and proved to be a reliable car. The only problem I can remember was a crunching noise when braking, which was due to the worn splines on the wheels and hubs. The first photograph was taken in 1952 and pictures my daughter standing next to the Dolomite.

Eventually the engine and bodywork required some attention so the car was laid-up in the late 1950s for repairs. I did some of the work myself but eventually handed it over to a mechanic to replace the running boards. It was whilst he was in the process of replacing the running boards that I had a telephone call from the police. They gave me the sad news that the mechanic had been killed when another vehicle he had been working on fell off its jacks. The Dolomite returned to my garage where it sat for the next 30 years or so.

I continued to be faithful to the marque owning several post-war Triumphs until they were no longer produced and had to move onto another manufacturer, Alfa.

It had always been my intention to return the Dolomite to the road but time waits for no one. Knowing that I was no longer able to fulfil my wish I reluctantly sold it to Don Impson, an 'old car' enthusiast. The second photograph shows me standing by the bonnet on 6th June 1993 the day it left my garage. Many of my neighbours were surprised to see what had been tucked away for all those years! Don has made a great job of restoring the Dolomite and was kind enough to take me for a ride in it, which I shall never forget.

Laurence Hole, Hertfordshire

Index

All the models that the Triumph Motor Company offered from the works are listed below. Unless they are featured in this book I have excluded the other body styles that were available from the many independent coachbuilders. Triumphs with special bodies fitted from new are annotated thus: *.

Index

My quest continues for photographs and memories of pre-war Triumph motor cars for inclusion in a possible third volume and I would pleased to hear from you if you can help.

If you wish to find out more about these cars please visit the Pre-1940 Triumph Owners Club website at 'www.pre-1940triumphownersclub.net'. Please note that in June 2010 it will have been decided whether the club changes its name to Pre-1940 Triumph Motor Club with effect from 1st January 2011. If this name change happens it is likely the website will similarly change to 'www.pre1940triumphmotorclub.net'.

PRE-1940
TRIUMPH
MOTOR CARS

from

FAMILY
PHOTOGRAPH
ALBUMS

'Volume 1'

Hopefully you will have enjoyed reading the Triumph memories in this book. If so you may be interested to know that 'Volume 1' is available direct from the author. This book was published in June 2005, contains 108 illustrated memories and is priced at £18.95 plus postage & packing.